LEFT BEHIND
Answered
Verse by Verse

To Jim and Emily Eubanks,
Your faithful service and songs
are an encouragement and
blessing to Penni and me.
In Jesus' love,
David

David A. Reed

Books by David A. Reed include:

Jehovah's Witnesses Ansswered Verse by Verse

Answering Jehovah's Witnesses Subject by Subject

Mormons Answered Verse by Verse

On the cover:

Spurgeon, Edwards, Wesley, Calvin, Tyndale, Luther, Wycliffe

ISBN: 978-1-4357-0873-0

Scripture References

JB   *The Jerusalem Bible* © 1968 by Darton, Longman & Todd, Ltd. and Doubleday & Company, Inc.

KJV   *King James Version*

LB   *The Living Bible* © 1971 by Tyndale House Publishers

NASB *New American Standard Bible* © 1995 Lockman Foundation

NIV   *The Holy Bible, New International Version* © 1973, 1978, 1984 by International Bible Society

NKJV *New King James Version, Holy Bible* © 1983 by Thomas Nelson, Inc.

RSV   *Revised Standard Version* © 1946, 1952 by Division of Christian Education of the Churches of Christ in the United States of America

Contents

Quotes Reflecting the Traditional Protestant Understanding

Preface

Shortly after putting faith in Jesus Christ, I began attending evangelical Christian churches—Baptist and Congregationalist—and that is where I first heard an exposition of the 'left behind' teaching.

Of course, the blockbuster novel by that title had not yet been written, because it was early in 1982 that I got down on my knees in the privacy of our kitchen, confessed myself a sinner, and told God in prayer that I accepted his son Jesus as my Savior and wanted to follow Christ as my Lord. Tim LaHaye and Jerry B. Jenkins didn't publish *Left Behind: A Novel of the Earth's Last Days* until 1995, but the end times beliefs expounded in that book were already commonly accepted in evangelical churches. Everyone I knew seemed to believe there would be a seven-year tribulation period climaxing the last days of this wicked world.

Little did I know then that this was a new teaching that had swept through the Church only decades before!

For years I never seriously took issue with this teaching, because it was held dearly, almost as an article of faith, by my fellow evangelicals. But it was always somewhat of a mystery to me, since I hadn't encountered it in my personal Bible reading. Perhaps it was one of the deeper things that takes a lot of study to grasp, I told myself. Or, perhaps my own thinking had been colored by thirteen years as a Jehovah's Witness, during which time I had been indoctrinated with *The Watchtower* magazine's eschatological views. In any case, I blamed my inability to grasp the seven-year tribulation on my own failure to study in depth the teaching and the biblical arguments behind it.

As a Jehovah's Witness I had been taught to believe that Jesus was the first angel God created, who was assigned to take on human flesh, to preach a message to mankind, to undergo a sacrificial death, and then to resume his role as the most prominent angel. We were taught that he returned invisibly in 1914, and that he would lead God's armies in the battle of Armageddon in 1975—a date that later had to be abandoned and explained away after the prediction proved false. (See my books *Jehovah's Witnesses Answered Verse by Verse* and *Answering Jehovah's Witnesses Subject by Subject*.) Having experienced intimately and first-hand the failure of such a false prophecy, I tended to be skeptical of prophetic speculation, even after I left the JWs and found sound Christian fellowship. Rejoicing in my Savior, I was content to trust in God for the outworking of the Bible's end times prophecies. It wasn't necessary for me to understand, only to trust and obey, since it was God who would bring these world-shaking events to pass as foretold in his inspired Word.

In the course of writing several more books on the Jehovah's Witnesses, I was forced to research more deeply into their roots in the Adventist movement. Prior to starting his own religion, Watch Tower founder Charles Taze Russell fellowshipped during the late 1860s and early 1870s with an Adventist sect that had Christ returning invisibly in 1874. Adventism, in turn, sprang from the die-hard followers of William Miller, a Baptist layman who had captured the imagination of believers in many churches with his predictions that Christ would return in March of 1843, later revised to March of 1844, and finally to the autumn of that year. A similar legacy of failed prophecy lay at the roots of Mormonism, I discovered when I teamed up with ex-Mormon John Farkas to research and write *Mormons Answered Verse by Verse* and other books on the history and errors of the Latter-day Saints.

Could the popular 'left behind' teachings be equally erroneous, I wondered? Certainly they were nothing like Mormonism with its polygamy and its plurality of gods; nor did they carry with them the heresy of the Jehovah's Witnesses who lower Christ from Creator to mere creature. Unlike these cultic movements hovering on the fringes of Christianity, the Left Behind books elevate the authority of Scripture and proclaim salvation through faith in Christ alone. Their greatest popularity is found within Bible-believing churches. Yet, the same could be said for the following of William Miller, himself a Baptist. His followers hailed from mainline Christian churches. But their trust in Miller's interpretations of the Bible's end times prophecies led to what historians have dubbed the "Great Disappointment."

Eventually, my research led me farther back, beyond these nineteenth century American religious movements, to the roots of modern Protestant thinking in the Reformation and the isolated back-to-the-Bible movements that preceded it. Here were believers who treasured their relationship with Christ more than life itself. Untold numbers were tortured to death, holding fast to their Lord. Many were burned at the stake. The truths in Scripture were more than mere Sunday morning entertainment for these humble yet courageous students of the Word. What did they say about a rapture that would leave unbelievers behind with a second chance to accept Christ during a seven-year tribulation?

They never heard of such a thing. The great Reformers Martin Luther and John Calvin both wrote extensively on the topic of the Antichrist, but the "man of sin" (2 Thess. 2:3) they described bore no resemblance whatsoever to the Nicolae Carpathia character of the Left Behind novels.

The Reformation saints who staked their very lives on the motto "Scripture Alone" saw in that precious Word of God neither a seven-year tribulation, nor a Carpathia-like world ruler presiding over it. What did they see? A very clear fulfillment of prophecy that fits the history of their times as well as today's headlines. The verse-by-verse discussion in this book will seek to be informed by the understanding of the Reformers.

Ultimately there were four factors weighing heavily on my heart that forced me to research and develop this manuscript:

First, a large portion of the population today assumes that *Left Behind* accurately presents what the Bible itself says. It does not.

Second, many Christians have come to believe that *Left Behind* represents the traditional beliefs of Protestant churches. It does not.

Third, those who accept the teachings of *Left Behind* find themselves looking for future events that would fit the fictional pattern. They believe that God's prophetic clock stopped, and won't start again until the Rapture. As a result, they miss the fulfillment of Bible prophecy in recent history and in today's headlines. This hinders their ability to follow Jesus' command to "be always on the watch." (Luke 21:36)

Finally, millions who read *Left Behind* are sitting on the fence of unbelief—both secular readers and half-hearted church attenders. Like the novel's nominally Christian commercial pilot Rayford Steele and assistant pastor Bruce Barnes, they go through the motions at church, but they don't truly trust in Christ or obey Him. Authors LaHaye and Jenkins show characters like this receiving a seven-year long "second chance" after Christ raptures believers. In the Gospels, however, Jesus warned over and over again that we should watch for his return to avoid severe punishment *at that time*. Do Jesus' parables—the wheat and the tares, the sheep and the goats, the ten talents, the wise and foolish virgins—offer a second chance for those surprised by the Master's return? If not, then *Left Behind* contradicts the clear teaching of Christ. Readers who are thus misled into postponing their decision for Christ could face an eternity without Him.

Our God is indeed the God of the second chance. Christ came to redeem sinners. Life usually affords each of us a second chance—in fact, *many* opportunities—to put our trust in Jesus Christ as our Savior and to obey him as our Lord. While still a teenager I rejected belief in God, and proclaimed myself an atheist for a number of years, but He had mercy on me and did not take that as my final decision. My grandmother was ninety-six years old when she finally read the Gospels and embraced Christ; I can only imagine how many chances she passed up before that. However, Scripture tells us that God's forbearance does not go on forever. Does the Bible teach that unbelievers will be 'left behind' for a seven-year-long second chance when Christ comes to take his faithful followers to heaven? That is the question this book will examine verse by verse.

Acknowledgements

The thoughts presented in this book are not new. Preachers and Bible readers have debated these issues over the centuries. I have simply attempted to arrange the traditional Protestant understanding in a verse by verse format to refute the misuse of Scripture in the Left Behind series. In addition to the quotes actually featured, every page could also be heavily footnoted, but that would favor the scholar rather than the average reader for whom this volume is intended.

My gratitude goes out to prolific author Rev. Dr. Francis Nigel Lee, Professor Emeritus of Systematic Theology at Queensland Presbyterian Theological Seminary, for his heavily footnoted book *John's Revelation Unveiled*, for his articles "Calvin on Islam" and "Luther on Islam and the Papacy," and for his kindness in responding to my questions via e-mail; also to my good friend Rev. Dr. Ronald Larson, long-time head of Baptist General Conference world missions and past president of Christian Medical Fellowship, for the resources he lent me from his personal library, especially his handwritten study notes.

I wish to express special appreciation to Rev. Joseph L. Haynes, pastor of Hague Gospel Church in Hague, Saskatchewan, Canada. Besides providing the extensive resources on his web sites Historicism.com and LastDays.ca, which I found very helpful while researching the material for this book, he also took the time to review early stages of the manuscript, offering insightful comments, corrections and contributions.

Of course, the opinions expressed in this book are my own, and whatever errors remain are my responsibility.

For this book's focus I must credit Eleanor ("Bootsie") Ashley, a cranberry-farming grandmother whose theology comes directly from the many Bibles she's worn out through her lifetime. When she saw the complex arguments I was assembling against Left Behind, she exclaimed with rock-solid confidence, "There's no second chance when Christ comes back. There's no second chance." From that point onward, I realized this teaching of a "second chance" was Left Behind's critical departure from Scripture and the main point to be refuted in this book.

And I truly thank my wife Penni for her help, prayer support and encouragement throughout this project, and for her active involvement in developing the manuscript.

Introduction

Do you expect Jesus Christ to return suddenly and invisibly, taking millions of Christian believers back to heaven with him, and leaving the rest of mankind to face a seven-year-long Tribulation presided over by an evil man called the Antichrist? Do you believe this Tribulation period will afford a 'second chance' for half-hearted churchgoers and for unbelievers who had rejected Christ prior to this?

If you came to that belief in recent years, the chances are that you or your religious instructors were influenced by the Left Behind series. Most likely you are unaware that this was not the teaching of Martin Luther, John Calvin, John Knox, Roger Williams and John Wesley—the founders of the Lutheran, Calvinist, Presbyterian, Baptist and Methodist traditions. Nor is it what Protestants in general believed for hundreds of years, from before the Reformation until the early twentieth century. Christian classics will be quoted throughout this book to establish traditional Protestant teaching, but first let's look more closely at Left Behind.

In 1995 California pastor Tim LaHaye and prolific writer Jerry B. Jenkins produced *Left Behind: A Novel of the Earth's Last Days*. The book's popularity soared, and it quickly gained a place on the *New York Times* Best Sellers list. It is still popular as I write these words in 2007, "the year the Left Behind series comes to an end" with release of the final volume in the series, according to the promotional web site at LeftBehind.com.

The first novel was soon followed by a sequel, *Tribulation Force: The Continuing Drama of Those Left Behind*. Next came *Nicolae: The Rise of Antichrist*. After that, the series continued to unfold its gripping end-times story: *Soul Harvest: The World Takes Sides* (No. 4), *Apollyon: The Destroyer Is Unleashed* (No. 5), *Assassins: Assignment: Jerusalem, Target: Antichrist* (No. 6), *The Indwelling: The Beast Takes Possession* (No. 7), *The Mark: The Beast Rules the World* (No. 8), *Desecration: Antichrist Takes the Throne* (No. 9), *The Remnant: On the Brink of Armageddon* (No. 10), *Armageddon: The Cosmic Battle of the Ages* (No. 11) and *Glorious Appearing: The End of Days* (No. 12). And then the series concluded (as of this writing) in April 2007 with *Kingdom Come: The Final Victory* (No. 13).

In October 2004, the publisher announced there would also be three prequels. The first of these, *The Rising: Antichrist Is Born–Before They Were Left Behind*, was released in March 2005 and was set decades before the original *Left Behind* novel. Then followed *The Regime: Evil Advances* and *The Rapture: In the Twinkling of an Eye*.

At last count more than forty-five million volumes have been sold in the series, plus another ten million in the Left Behind Kids Series, and ten million more related items. There are additional volumes in a Military Series, a Political Series, a complete illustrated Graphic Novels Series, more than a dozen apologetic works in the Nonfiction Series, daily devotional volumes, audio tapes, videos, CD-ROMs, calendars, greeting cards, and so on. Simple arithmetic reveals this to be a billion dollar industry. (Multiply sixty-five million items times $15.00 each, and the result is roughly $1 billion.) No wonder *Left Behind* has had such widespread impact on the beliefs of so many people!

Are readers guilty of mistaking the authors' intentions and acting presumptuously when they take these fiction stories seriously and allow the novels to mold their thinking on biblical matters? No, this is what the authors intended. A "note from Dr. Tim LaHaye" at the end of the last novel in the series says, "Jerry and I felt uniquely led of God to take on this challenging task of presenting what we believe is the truth of end times prophecy in fiction form. Our prayer was that it would take admittedly complex and often confusing elements of Scripture and help them come to life in your eyes. . . . we believe what we have portrayed here will happen someday." (*Kingdom Come: The Final Victory*, pages 355-356)

In many churches the Left Behind view of the end times is accepted as a virtual extension of the Gospel. To question its theology is to question orthodoxy itself. Many Christians appear unaware that opposing views exist at all within the Church among sincere Bible believers. Tim LaHaye and Jerry B. Jenkins have been heralded as "The New Prophets of Revelation" on the cover of *Newsweek* magazine (May 24, 2004). So, is there anyone in the Christian community who has the stature to challenge their teaching on the end times?

I would nominate Martin Luther and John Calvin. These giants of the Protestant Reformation taught quite differently concerning the Tribulation and the Antichrist. As will be shown in the discussion of Daniel 9:24-27 below, a key passage of central importance that Luther and Calvin applied to Jesus Christ, is turned around in Left Behind to apply to the Antichrist, instead—a dramatic reversal that changes its entire meaning. Moreover, the Reformers saw the Antichrist rising from the ashes of the Roman Empire and ruling much of the world in which they lived—a two-horned Antichrist that continues to rule today and to influence the lives of billions worldwide. If Luther and Calvin are correct, the Left Behind series actually helps the present Antichrist by concealing his identity and telling readers to look for someone else in the future, someone like their Nicolae Carpathia character.

Others who side with Calvin and Luther against the Left Behind view include William Tyndale (English Bible translator), Jonathan Edwards (Congregationalist missionary in colonial America), Roger Williams (the first Baptist pastor in America), John Knox (early Scottish Presbyterian), John Wesley (Methodist founding father), John Huss (martyred by the Inquisition) and John Wycliffe (Bible translator). All of these respected teachers will be quoted repeatedly in the pages below to establish the traditional Protestant view, which was taught in evangelical churches until a mere hundred years ago. Must the teachings of all these Christian leaders be rejected and tossed aside, in order to make room for the contrary teachings of Tim LaHaye and Jerry Jenkins?

Of course, LaHaye and Jenkins did not originate the view of the end times that they portray in their fiction books. They have merely taken the lead in spreading and popularizing this viewpoint. Where, then, did the "left behind" teachings come from? Not surprisingly, they originated in one of the nineteenth century religious movements. Around the time when Joseph Smith was writing the Book of Mormon, and William Miller was laying the early foundations of the Adventist movement, preacher John Nelson Darby began developing the theology of dispensationalism.

Born in England in 1800, Darby graduated from Trinity College in Dublin, Ireland, and took up Christian ministry. He helped form a small fellowship in Dublin that eventually branched out to Plymouth, England and came to be called "Plymouth Brethren." It was to this group that Darby proclaimed the seven-year tribulation concept as part of his overall teaching of dispensationalism—the theory that God's dealings with mankind are defined by a series of fixed time periods or *dispensations* spanning the whole of human history. The seven-year tribulation is merely one of many such time periods that are marked out on dispensationalist time charts.

Darby spent a couple decades modifying and refining dispensations to fully develop the theory of dispensationalism. At first the teaching was confined to the Plymouth Brethren, but it was soon picked up by others.

By the late 1800s major Protestant seminaries were coming under its influence, and dispensational timelines and tables were being published by a number of groups. I first encountered such charts myself in *The Divine Plan of the Ages*, the first volume of the *Millennial Dawn/Studies in the Scriptures* series by Charles Taze Russell, founder of the Watch Tower Society, the parent organization of the modern Jehovah's Witnesses.

But dispensationalism did not widely influence the thinking of Christian lay people until it was popularized through the *Scofield Reference Bible*. According to researcher Richard R. Reiter, Congregationalist pastor Cyrus I. Scofield came into a financial relationship with "some wealthy Plymouth Brethren." They enabled him and other pretribulationists to start the Sea Cliff Bible Conference in 1901 on Long Island, New York. (*Three Views on the Rapture: Pre-, Mid-, or Post-Tribulation* by Gleason L. Archer, Jr., Paul D. Feinberg, Douglas J. Moo, and Richard R. Reiter [Zondervan, 1996]) Less than a decade later Scofield incorporated Darby's ideas in the notes of his study Bible published in 1909. This gave Darby's teachings leverage to color the way many Bible readers understood Scripture.

Considerable controversy surrounds the question of where Darby got his new ideas. Some researchers claim he borrowed them from the sermons and writings of controversial contemporary pastor Edward Irving. Others, that he learned his concept of the Rapture from another contemporary, Margaret MacDonald, a young woman who claimed to have seen a vision of the end times.

Many writers have traced these interpretations back to the writings of the Counter-Reformation. When the early Reformers began pointing to the pope of Rome as the Antichrist, the Roman Catholic Church launched a campaign to defend the papacy. In 1590 Jesuit priest Francisco Ribera (1537-1591) published a commentary on Revelation titled *In Sacrum Beati Ioannis Apostoli, & Evangelistiae Apocalypsin Commentarji,* in which he taught that there would be a future end-times Antichrist. Another Jesuit priest, Manuel De Lacunza, later wrote *La Venida del Mesias en Gloria y Magestad* in Spanish under a Jewish pen name, Juan Josafa Ben-Ezra. It was published in a number of places during the early 1800s. This book countered the Protestant identification of the Antichrist with the papacy by arguing that there would be future antichrists instead. Darby's contemporary pastor Edward Irving translated Lacunza's book into English, added his own lengthy preface, and had it published in London in 1827 as *Preliminary Discourse to the Work of Ben Ezra entitled the Coming of Messiah in Glory and Majesty.* Did Darby actually derive his teachings from these sources? The matter is open to debate.

Supporters see foregleams of Darby's teachings in the writings of early Church penman Irenaeus and his disciple Hippolytus, who reigned as bishop of Rome from 200 to 235 A.D., but there is no clear evidence connecting Darby with these sources. In fact, the advocates of a variety of other end times interpretations point to other early Church writers to support their views as well. The problem is that those associated with the early Church during the centuries following the Apostles held a variety of views, just like Christians today. After quoting many of them, one researcher spoke of "the variety and complexity of patristic views concerning the Antichrist." ("Antichrist in the Early Church" by William C. Weinrich in the April/July 1985 issue of *Concordia Theological Quarterly*) So, the writings of the "Early Church Fathers" can be used to support a variety of interpretations. The writings that truly count are those found in the Holy Scriptures. And it is to these that this book appeals in its verse by verse discussion.

Whatever the case may be as to John Nelson Darby's sources, the notes he inspired in the 1909 Scofield Reference Bible gave the pre-tribulation rapture theory widespread circulation among Bible readers. A host of Bible teachers, pastors and non-fiction writers kept the theory alive during most of the twentieth century. Then, more than a generation after Scofield, the novel *Left Behind* by LaHaye and Jenkins spread the teaching among readers of popular fiction.

Some knowingly set aside the teachings of Luther, Calvin and the other Reformers, to accept this new teaching. Pastor Chuck Smith of Calvary Chapel writes, "The story goes that in a meeting in England a woman began to exhort the Church through the gift of prophecy, and she said that the Lord was going to take His Church out and save it from the wrath to come. We're told that men like Darby and Scofield then began to popularize this view. . . . Why would the Lord reveal it to Luther, Calvin, or any of the Reformation Church leaders? They weren't living in the age when the Church was to be taken out." (From an article titled "The Tribulation and the Church" by Chuck Smith at http://www3.calvarychapel.com/library/smith-chuck/books/ttatc.htm) So, this supporter of Left Behind theology supports Margaret MacDonald's claimed new revelation, over and above the wisdom of the Reformation.

Rather than look to supposed new revelation, the Reformers lifted high the standard of *Scripture Alone*. Luther and Calvin lived in the 1500s and Margaret MacDonald in the 1800s. Was she living "in the age when the Church was to be taken out" more so than they? Nearly two hundred years have passed since she spoke. Moreover, isn't Scripture the standard by which any claimed new revelation would have to be judged?

In any case, it is clear that "dispensationalism is not a part of the historic faith of the church," the conclusion reached by Clarence B. Bass, Associate Professor of Systematic Theology at Bethel Theological Seminary, in his book *Backgrounds to Dispensationalism: Its Historical Genesis and Ecclesiastical Implications.* (page 155) It is a relatively new teaching.

A lot of good is accomplished when a Christian book makes its way onto *The New York Times* best-sellers list. The general public is reminded, once again, of the Gospel message and its relevance to the modern world. But William Miller's prophecies concerning 1843 and 1844 likewise drew public attention to the expected return of Christ, only to culminate in public scorn and ridicule when those years came and went. That prophetic stirring was more than just a theological error within Bible-believing churches; it also resulted in personal disaster for untold numbers of believers. In 1843 "seventeen persons were admitted to the Lunatic Asylum in Worcester, Mass., who had become deranged in consequence of the expectation that the Lord Jesus was about to appear," according to Albert Barnes in his *Notes on the New Testament*, 2 Thess. 2:2. The message of *Left Behind* can't fail in that sense, of course, because no precise dates are set for the events in the story. But what if the Reformers were correct, rather than Darby and Scofield? What if, as Luther and Calvin indicated, the Antichrist is already ruling, and the 'left behind' interpretation keeps people from recognizing him? What if the return of Christ and the rapture are accompanied immediately by the pouring out of God's wrath on this wicked world—without giving those who reject Christ the seven-year-long 'second chance' promised by Left Behind?

Ultimately, the matter revolves around faithfulness to Scripture. How does the end-times vision of *Left Behind* stack up against the Word of God? The aim of this book is to make that comparison verse by verse.

Schools of Thought on Prophecy

The reader has a right to know, up front, the viewpoint presented in this book.

Christian writers typically hold membership in churches or denominations that officially espouse a particular system of belief. Their church's Statement of Faith may spell out a view of end times prophecy or, if it is silent on these matters, there may still be a viewpoint that is nearly universal or at least prevalent among the members. The books penned by these men generally reflect their affiliation. In my own case, however, my religious affiliation has long been with churches where Left Behind theology prevails, but my personal Bible reading and research will no longer allow me to go along with that teaching.

Among Bible-believing Christians there are several well-defined schools of thought on end times prophecy.

The *preterist* view interprets most 'end times' passages in Scripture as applying to events in the first century. Preterists see Jesus' predictions in Matthew chapter 24 as foretelling the destruction of Jerusalem and its temple in 70 A.D., and John's Revelation as fulfilled during the reign of the Roman Empire—with little or no future application.

The *idealist* or *spiritual* view sees almost no chronological fulfillment of prophecy in historical or future events, but rather interprets the prophecies as pictorial of the timeless struggle of good-versus-evil. This view is more popular in liberal churches and among some seminary professors who have grown dissatisfied with the Left Behind interpretations. Although some proponents of this school of thought expect Christ to return physically to Earth at the time of the Last Judgment, the idealist approach is to draw principles from prophecy to apply in our every-day lives, rather than to look for God's dramatic intervention in the course of history.

The *dispensational futurist* view is that most of the events predicted by Jesus in the Gospels and foretold in the book of Revelation will occur in the future, primarily during a seven-year tribulation period ruled over by the Antichrist. This is the Left Behind view that prevails in evangelical churches today.

The *historicist* view sees the fulfillment of prophecy throughout the course of history, with some events occurring in the first century, some up to and including the present time, and others in the future. The historicist view prevailed in Protestant churches from the time of the Reformation until it gradually declined in popularity during the late 1800's and early 1900's.

Dispensational futurism supplanted historicism among evangelicals when the *Scofield Reference Bible* popularized John Nelson Darby's theory, which divided earth's history into a series of dispensations and consigned the apocalyptic prophecies to a future seven-year tribulation period. The Left Behind series further popularized this view by fictionalizing it for mass readership.

Within preterism, idealism, futurism and historicism there are, as might be expected, a number of variations with respect to many details—some quite significant. Preterists war among themselves, for example, with Partial Preterists accusing Full Preterists of heresy for teaching that even Christ's final Coming and the resurrection of the righteous and the unrighteous have already occurred. There are both dispensational and non-dispensational futurists, although the latter form a tiny minority. Historicism, because it looks for prophetic fulfillment throughout the span of human history, affords the greatest range of differences. Unlike preterists who focus on one century, and dispensationalists who focus on seven years, historicists have a much wider range of events to choose from when looking for prophetic fulfillments, since they take the whole of human history into consideration.

In this book I turn to the traditional Protestant understanding of Scripture to offer verse-by-verse responses to the popular new dispensationalist teaching that swept over the churches during the past century. Since the traditional Protestant view is historicist, *LEFT BEHIND Answered Verse by Verse* would be classified as historicist in its approach.

Some readers may be intimidated by the many complex theories in the field of eschatology—the study of end times prophecy—so I should address here the concerns of those who feel they may be 'getting in over their head.' Folks who have come to faith in Christ by reading the Bible alone do not need this book, or any other book on the end times. The divine Author of the Holy Scriptures did not fall so far short of getting his message across, that an explanatory supplement would be required. Nor did he write the Bible for a hierarchy of experts to read, and then in turn present its message to the common man. God's Word comes across loud and clear to the farmer, fisherman or housewife who reads it after a hard day's work. And the passages that speak of the return of Christ are no exception. Just as with my earlier works *Jehovah's Witnesses Answered Verse by Verse* and *Mormons Answered Verse by Verse*, the need for this book arises due to the popularity of certain of teachings that have been imposed upon the Bible from outside—teachings that purport to clarify Scripture, but that actually distort its message. In the case of Left Behind the distortion is not as extreme as in the teachings addressed by my other books, but it is a subtle twisting of what the Bible says about Christ's return, a twisting that could prove deadly for some, and that needs to be answered verse by verse.

What 'Left Behind' teaches

The central teaching of the Left Behind series is that Christ returns twice, and that this gives those who reject Christ before the Rapture a 'second chance.'

The novels show Christ returning first invisibly to rapture the Church to heaven, then seven years later to destroy the wicked and to take "Tribulation saints" to heaven. The volume *Nicolae: The Rise of Antichrist* summarizes this teaching from the post-Rapture perspective as "belief in the one true God, that Jesus is his Son, that he came back, and that he's coming back again." (p. 380) In their nonfiction work *Are We Living in the End Times?* authors LaHaye and Jenkins describe Christ's return as "two totally different events. One is a select coming for His church, a great source of comfort for those involved; the other is a public appearance when every eye shall see Him, a great source of regret and mourning for those whose Day of Judgment has come. . . . Seven years would allow time for all these things and the Tribulation to take place." (p. 103)

Second Chance is the title of one of the novels in the children's series *Left Behind: The Kids*. And in their nonfiction book *Are We Living in the End Times*, LaHaye and Jenkins state specifically that the seven-year interval grants this second chance to those "left behind after the Rapture" because they had "rejected God's offer of salvation." (page 158)

Verse-by-verse Answers—Old Testament

The reader may be tempted to skip past this discussion of Old Testament verses, to get the last word on prophecy from the New Testament. This book is designed to allow that. However, a word of caution is in order.

The Old Testament is key to understanding the New, especially in matters of prophecy. The "beasts" of Revelation cannot be identified correctly by a reader unfamiliar with the beasts Daniel saw in his visions. Jesus' sermon on the end times and his Second Coming rested heavily on the assumption that his listeners already knew what Moses wrote about the future of the Jewish people and what Daniel wrote about the "abomination of desolation." (Matt. 24:15 KJV)

Trying to understand the New Testament's end times prophecies without first examining what the Old Testament said on the same matters can lead only to misinterpretations and confusion.

Genesis 7:7-21

> And Noah went in, and his sons, and his wife, and his sons' wives with him, into the ark, because of the waters of the flood. ...and the Lord shut him in. ...And all flesh died that moved upon the earth, both of fowl, and of cattle, and of beast, and of every creeping thing that creepeth upon the earth, and every man. (KJV)

The fate of those left behind when Noah and his family took refuge in the Ark is very significant to end times theology, because Jesus said the end of this world would be the same: "And as it was in the days of Noah, so shall it be also in the days of the Son of man. They did eat, they drank, they married wives, they were given in marriage, until the day that Noah entered into the ark, and the flood came, and destroyed them all." (Luke 17:26-27 KJV) Those left behind were destroyed.

Bible commentator Matthew Henry (1662 – 1714) understood there was no 'second chance' for that wicked world. He wrote, "the shutting of this door set up a partition wall between him [Noah] and all the world besides. God shut the door, 1. To secure him, and keep him safe in the ark. The door must be shut very close, lest the waters should break in and sink the ark, and very fast, lest any without should break it down. ... To exclude all others, and keep them for ever out." (*Matthew Henry's Commentary*) There was no second chance for those left behind when God shut the door. They were kept out "for ever."

Similar to the pre-deluge society Noah had lived in, today's world has abandoned the righteousness of God to follow every wicked way. "And God saw that the wickedness of man was great in the earth and that every imagination of the thoughts of his heart was only evil continually. And it repented the Lord that he had made man on the earth, and it grieved him at his heart. And the Lord said, I will destroy man whom I have created from the face of the earth..." (Gen. 6:5-7 KJV) As God looks down upon our modern society with its movie star sex goddesses, its high rate of promiscuity and divorce, its criminal and military violence, and its denial of his creatorship in favor of the theory of evolution, it must similarly grieve him at his heart. Will the Creator again assert his sovereign right to wipe clean his creation?

Jesus leaves no doubt: "As it was in the days of Noah, so shall it be also in the days of the Son of man." (Luke 17:26 KJV) He will again take his people to safety, and will destroy those left behind. Just as there was no seven-year reprieve for those left behind when the Ark floated above the flood waters, so there will be none for those left when Christians are taken to be with the Lord at the end of this world.

Genesis 19:15-16, 24

> And when the morning arose, then the angels hastened Lot...and they brought him forth and set him outside of the city. ...Then the Lord rained upon Sodom and Gomorrah brimstone and fire from the Lord out of heaven; and he overthrew those cities, and all the plain, and all the inhabitants of the cities. (KJV)

What happened to those who were left behind when holy angels led righteous Lot and his family out of Sodom? Everyone left behind was killed.

This prefigured what will happen to those left behind when Christ raptures the Church. Jesus said, "Also as it was in the days of Lot; they did eat, they drank, they bought, they sold, they planted, they built; but the same day that Lot went out of Sodom, it rained fire and brimstone from heaven, and destroyed them all. Even thus shall it be in the day when the Son of man is revealed." (Luke 17:28-30 KJV)

Was there a seven-year delay after the angels took Lot to safety? No, Lot was taken out of the city and "the same day" all of those left behind were killed.

Writing in the early 1700s, Matthew Henry again got the point. Commenting on Luke 17:28-30, he wrote:

> ". . . they continued in their security and sensuality, till the threatened judgment came. Until the day that Noah entered into the ark, and Lot went out of Sodom, nothing said or done to them served to alarm or awaken them. Note, Though the stupidity of sinners in a sinful way is as strange as it is without excuse, yet we are not to think it strange, for it is not without example. It is the old way that wicked men have trodden, that have gone slumbering to hell, as if their damnation slumbered while they did. . . .That they were surprised with the ruin which they would not fear, and were swallowed up in it, to their unspeakable horror and amazement. ...In like manner, when Jesus Christ shall come to judge the world, at the end of time, sinners will be found in the same secure and careless posture, altogether regardless of the judgment approaching, which will therefore come upon them as a snare." (*Matthew Henry's Commentary on the Whole Bible*)

Matthew Henry did not expect the disobedient to get a 'second chance' at Christ's return.

After referring to Sodom and Gomorrah and saying, "even thus shall it be," Jesus went on to describe the Rapture: "two women shall be grinding together; the one shall be taken, and the other left. Two men shall be in the field; the one shall be taken, and the other left." How will it be at the Rapture? "As it was in the days of Lot," Jesus declared. (Luke 17:30-36, 28 KJV)

Everyone knows the sin of Sodom. Our word "sodomy" comes

straight from that city's name. When Lot entertained visitors in his home, two angels sent by God, "Sodomites young and old from all over the city...surrounded the house and shouted to Lot, 'Bring out those men to us so we can rape them.'" Prior to that the Bible reported that "the people of Sodom and Gomorrah are utterly evil, and that everything they do is wicked." (Gen. 19:4-5, 18:20 *Living Bible*)

Like Sodom and Gomorrah, our modern society has become pervaded with homosexual perversion. It is difficult to visit a movie theater, turn on a television set, or read a newspaper without encountering it. Elementary school textbooks feature "families" with two fathers or two mothers instead of the traditional married couple. Practicing homosexuals serve as clergy in countless churches. There is public debate over whether or not to sanctify "gay marriage," but the practice of homosexuality is already protected nearly everywhere by antidiscrimination legislation. Politicians jostle each other to march in Gay Pride parades. God, however, does discriminate.

Has this world yet reached the point where Sodom and Gomorrah have been recreated worldwide? When that stage is reached, it is difficult to imagine that the God who brought destruction on those ancient cities will simply turn his head and allow it to go on this time. When he does step in again to put a stop to the sin of Sodom, Jesus assures us it will be much the same as the first time. People who belong to Christ will be taken, and those who are left behind will be killed. Will the destruction come seven years later, as the authors of the Left Behind novels would have us believe? Jesus said, "the same day that Lot went out of Sodom, it rained fire and brimstone from heaven, and destroyed them all. Even thus shall it be..." (Luke 17:29-30 KJV)

Isaiah 11:11-12

> Then it will happen on that day that the Lord will again recover the second time with His hand the remnant of His people, who will remain, from Assyria, Egypt, Pathros, Cush, Elam, Shinar, Hamath, and from the islands of the sea. And He will lift up a standard for the nations and assemble the banished ones of Israel, and will gather the dispersed of Judah from the four corners of the earth. (NASB)

The restoration of the Jewish people to the Promised Land is an amazing fulfillment of prophecy that should convince even the most skeptical that the Bible is a divinely inspired book of true prophecy. As Jesus foretold during the Roman occupation, "And they shall fall by the edge of the sword and be led away captive into all nations: and Jerusalem shall be trodden down of the Gentiles, until the times of the Gentiles be fulfilled." (Luke 21:24 KJV) And as Isaiah and other Old Testament writers foretold, they would later be restored to their ancient homeland. This actually happened in 1948, with the re-establishment of the state of Israel, nearly two thousand years after Jesus spoke and some 2500 years after the Hebrew prophets foretold this event. Who could deny God's hand in such a seemingly impossible fulfillment? Supporters of Left Behind theology!

Yes, they deny that Isaiah's words above have yet been fulfilled. They expect the fulfillment will occur when the Jews will *again* be scattered worldwide and will *again* be restored to the land of Israel, and they use Isaiah's words above ("the second time") to justify this teaching. In *The Truth Behind Left Behind* (with Introduction by *Left Behind* author Tim LaHaye) authors Mark Hitchcock and Thomas Ice postulate "Two End-Time Regatherings" and declare that "during the Tribulation period, the Jewish people will be scattered over the face of the earth for the final time." To 'prove' this they present charts and tables to contrast what they see as "The Present (First) Regathering" and "The Permanent (Second) Regathering" (pages 61-64).

Charts and tables are needed to argue for such a theory, because people left alone to read their Bibles would never come to this conclusion. In fact, the argument is so complex that even its proponents get confused and trip themselves up while presenting it. For example, Hitchcock and Ice declare "MODERN ISRAEL IS A WORK OF GOD" in an all-caps heading on page 58 of their book, and then contradict that statement five pages later in a chart labeling "the present (first) regathering" as "Man's work (secular)" as opposed to "the permanent (second) regathering" which is "God's work (spiritual)." (page 63)

Actually, there is no need for such convoluted reasoning to explain why Isaiah would speak above concerning Israel being gathered a "second time." During the Babylonian captivity in Old Testament times Jews were to be found scattered across that ancient empire, which ruled much of the known world at that time. When the Medo-Persian rulers who conquered Babylon later sent the Jews back to the Promised Land, this was the *first* time they were regathered; the modern return that culminated in restoration of the nation of Israel in 1948 was the *second* time.

Was the 1948 return just "man's work," not God's? Was it a product of political Zionism, rather than God's intervention? Well, to secular observers in ancient Medo-Persia who witnessed the decrees of king Cyrus and emperor Artaxerxes on behalf of the Jews, the actions of those rulers may have appeared political, but the Scriptures make it clear that God's hand was in the matter. Similarly today, Jewish Zionism may have been a political movement, but the modern restoration of the state of Israel after two thousand years could only have been accomplished through divine intervention.

Rejecting this obvious fulfillment of prophecy, and looking instead for *another* end-times restoration, smacks of the same kind of reasoning that leads unbelieving Jews to reject Christ and look for *another* Messiah.

Yes, God does "recover the second time with His hand the remnant of His people" as Isaiah says. The first time was five hundred years before Christ, and the second time is marked by the modern restoration of Israel in 1948. There is no biblical basis for expecting 'two end-time regatherings' as Left Behind teaches, with Israel to be scattered again and gathered again during a seven-year tribulation.

Jeremiah 30:7

> Alas! for that day is great, so that none is like it: it is even the time of Jacob's trouble; but he shall be saved out of it. (KJV)

Quoting from and commenting on their own novel, LaHaye and Jenkins say, "'the last forty-two months of this seven years of tribulation . . . That last half of the seven years is called the Great Tribulation.' . . . Jeremiah the prophet had called it 'the time of Jacob's trouble.'" (*Are We Living in the End Times?*, pages 145-146) The Left Behind novels portray the last half of their fictional tribulation period as a time when the Antichrist persecutes the Jews. Interestingly, the authors go on in their next sentence to say that the impact on the Jews would be "far worse" than "the Holocaust of Adolph Hitler in the twentieth century." (p. 146)

It is hard to imagine anything worse than the Holocaust in which six million Jews were systematically slaughtered. Must we look to the future for "the time of Jacob's trouble"? Jeremiah's description so aptly fits the Holocaust itself, that there is no need to look elsewhere for the fulfillment.

The message of Jeremiah chapter 30 starts out with this proclamation: "The days are coming,' declares the LORD , 'when I will bring my people Israel and Judah back from captivity and restore them to the land I gave their forefathers to possess,' says the LORD." (vs. 3 NIV) History undeniably records that the modern state of Israel was established in 1948. Did Jeremiah speak of *Jacob's time of trouble* occurring before that (as in the case of the Holocaust) or after that (as in the case of Left Behind's future tribulation)? Verses 7 and 8 indicate that the Jews would face a terrible time of trouble, then be rescued out of it, and thereafter be free from foreign domination: "How awful that day will be! None will be like it. It will be a time of trouble for Jacob, but he will be saved out of it. 'In that day,' declares the LORD Almighty, 'I will break the yoke off their necks and will tear off their bonds; no longer will foreigners enslave them.'" (NIV) So, Jeremiah showed the 'time of trouble' coming *before* the restoration of Israel.

Did the Lord give Jeremiah a preview of the events of 1941 through 1948? Was the prophet writing of the demonic attempt to exterminate the Jewish people, followed by their return to the Promised Land, with the establishment of a strong national government of their own? Perhaps. Or does "the time of Jacob's trouble" predict an era instead of a day? Does it point to the scattering of the Jews during most of the past two thousand years as the 'time of trouble'? Again, perhaps. The Lord will make all things clear in His time.

Whatever the case, 'Jacob's time of trouble' can be used to support Left Behind's seven-year tribulation theory only by wresting it out of context. It occurs *before* the restoration of the Jews to the Promised Land, not afterwards. And it is *Jacob*'s time of trouble, not a tribulation on the whole world.

Ezekiel 38:3-16

Thus saith the Lord: Behold I am against thee, O Gog,

the chief prince of Meshech and Tubal ... in latter years
thou shalt come into the land that is brought back from the
sword, and is gathered out of many peoples, against the
mountains of Israel ... And thou shalt come from thy place
out of the north parts, thou, and many peoples with thee,
all of them riding upon horses, a great company, and a
mighty army; And thou shalt come up against my people of
Israel, like a cloud to cover the land; it shall be in the latter
days... (KJV)

The original *Left Behind* novel, volume 1 of the series, begins soon after a strange war has taken place. The characters reminisce how Russia launched a massive air attack against Israel, only to have all of its planes mysteriously destroyed. The implication is that this is the attack by Gog, "prince of Rosh" according to many translations of Ezekiel 38:3. However, the connection between *Rosh* and *Russia* is dubious, even though the two sound alike in English. The Hebrew word *rosh* occurs 598 times in Scripture, according to *Strong's Concordance*, and none of those occurrences refer to a people or nation; rather, it is a common noun meaning *head, chief, top, beginning* or something similar, depending on the context.

Although *The New Scofield Reference Bible* (1967 edition) says *chief prince* in the main text and *prince of Rosh* only in a marginal note, the footnote says, "The reference is to the powers in the north of Europe, headed by Russia. ... The entire prophecy belongs to the yet future day of the Lord."

Ezekiel said Gog would attack a future restored state of Israel in the distant future, a land "whose people were gathered from many nations to the mountains of Israel, which had long been desolate." (38:8 NIV) This description could fit the modern state of Israel, populated by Jews who returned to the Promised Land from Europe and the Americas, and even from Russia itself.

The prophet adds that Gog would have allies. "Persia, Cush and Put will be with them, all with shields and helmets, also Gomer with all its troops, and Beth Togarmah from the far north with all its troops—the many nations with you." (38:5-6 NIV) So, the attackers would include Iran (Persia) and "many" other nations. The Apostle John's *Apocalypse* uses similar language to refer to *all* the nations—"the nations in the four corners of the earth—Gog and Magog." (Revelation 20:8)

Throughout the years of the Cold War it was the Soviet Union (primarily Russia) that took the lead in attacking Israel in the United Nations, along with the Arab states. Huge majorities passed countless General Assembly resolutions condemning the Jewish state. Why didn't the U.N. take military action against Israel on the scale of the Korean conflict? America's veto in the Security Council precluded such an attack.

However, the nations surrounding the restored modern state of Israel—its immediate neighbors—did attack more than once over the years. In 1948, after Israel declared its independence, it was invaded by the armies of Egypt, Syria, Transjordan (later Jordan), Lebanon, Iraq and Saudi Arabia. Local Palestinian Arab forces also fought the Jews. In 1967 the forces of Egypt, Jordan, Syria and Iraq massed on Israel's borders in obvious preparation for a massive attack, but Israel struck first preemptively in what came to be called the Six Day War. In the War of Attrition (1969-70) Israel's neighbors precipitated frequent clashes along the borders and the 1967 cease-fire lines, with additional guerilla action inside Israel itself. In the Yom Kippur War (or Ramadan War from the Arab perspective) of 1973, the forces of Egypt, Syria and Iraq again attacked the Jewish state.

Although initially backing Israel during the 1948 war and the truce that followed, the early 1950s saw the Soviet Union switch to supporting the Arab states. Russia played a major role in the later multi-national attacks against Israel.

The Russians reportedly supplied much of the sophisticated military equipment used by the Arab side in the 1967 Six Day War. In the 1969-1970 War of Attrition, the Soviet Union participated actively in Egypt's air defense by providing military hardware and thousands of "advisors." According to information supplied by the Israel Defense Forces and published in the Jewish Virtual Library, Russians actually piloted Mig fighter planes, operated the sophisticated radar installations, and launched surface-to-air missiles against Israeli planes. The IAF reported shooting down five Russian pilots. (http://www.jewishvirtuallibrary.org/jsource/Society_&_Culture/69iaf.html)

Was Gog's attack in Ezekiel a portrayal of Russia waging war against Israel by proxy through all of its Arab neighbors? Could it be that Ezekiel's prophecy was fulfilled in Russia's mobilizing the United Nations—all the nations of the world—to condemn Israel? At last

28

count, there were well over three hundred General Assembly resolutions and more than fifty Security Council resolutions concerning Israel, the vast majority of them condemning the actions of the Jewish state. (Most of these were supported by Russia and its Arab allies.) Or did the prophet write of a full-scale attack on Israel by Russia and a limited group of allies? Or was Ezekiel speaking of a move against Israel by all the nations of the world, a final attack that triggers God's wrath at Armageddon?

Time will tell. Christians will be in a better position to identify the correct interpretation as the fulfillment of end times prophecy continues to play out. Whatever the case, however, there is nothing in this passage to indicate that the events described lead up to a seven-year tribulation as described in *Left Behind*.

Daniel 2:39

> After you, another kingdom will rise, inferior to yours. Next, a third kingdom, one of bronze, will rule over the whole earth. Dan. 2:39 (NIV)

According to the authors of the Left Behind series the second chapter of Daniel predicts a future world government like their fictional "Global Community" ruled over by a man like their character Nicolae Carpathia, the Antichrist. "The governments of the world will relinquish their sovereignty to one head, an international world leader," say LaHaye and Jenkins in their nonfiction book *Are We Living in the End Times*. "This is clearly predicted in ... Daniel 2." (page 169)

Is that really what Daniel wrote? Was he predicting that a United Nations Secretary General like Carpathia would become world Potentate with all the nations surrendering their sovereignty to him? Daniel did use the expression "rule over the whole earth"—but in reference to the Greek empire of Alexander the Great, not as a prediction of Left Behind's "Global Community."

The second chapter of Daniel, where LaHaye sees such a prediction, actually centers on a strange dream that Babylonian king Nebuchadnezzar dreamed in the seventh century B.C., and which the

Hebrew prophet interpreted for him.

The dream had left the monarch troubled, but he could not recall anything about it. He summoned "the magicians, and the astrologers, and the sorcerers, and the Chaldeans," (Dan. 2:2 KJV) who were in his service and demanded that they make known to him both the dream and its interpretation. They, in turn, asked the king to tell them what he had seen in the dream. If only he would tell them about the dream, they would be glad to interpret it. That would be an easy matter. But, alas, the king could not remember. He insisted that his wise men give him *both* the dream *and* its interpretation. Even under the furious ruler's sentence of death, none of them could tell Nebuchadnezzar what he himself had forgotten.

Then Daniel came on the scene. With God's help he told the king exactly what he had dreamed:

"You looked, O king, and there before you stood a large statue—an enormous, dazzling statue, awesome in appearance. The head of the statue was made of pure gold, its chest and arms of silver, its belly and thighs of bronze, its legs of iron, its feet partly of iron and partly of baked clay. While you were watching, a rock was cut out, but not by human hands. It struck the statue on its feet of iron and clay and smashed them. Then the iron, the clay, the bronze, the silver and the gold were broken to pieces at the same time and became like chaff on a threshing floor in the summer. The wind swept them away without leaving a trace. But the rock that struck the statue became a huge mountain and filled the whole earth." (verses 31-35 NIV)

How could he tell what someone else dreamed, when even the dreamer himself had forgotten? Daniel attributed this special knowledge to the "God in heaven who revealeth secrets." (Dan. 2:28 KJV) Nebuchadnezzar recalled the dream, of course, after Daniel reminded him, and therefore recognized Daniel's authority to interpret it as well. The Jewish prophet explained it to him this way:

"You, O king... You are that head of gold. After you, another kingdom will rise, inferior to yours. Next, a third kingdom, one of bronze, will rule over the whole earth. Finally, there will be a fourth kingdom, strong as iron—for iron breaks and smashes everything—and as iron breaks things to pieces, so it will crush and break all the others. Just as you saw that the feet and toes were partly of baked clay and partly of iron, so this will be a divided kingdom; yet it will have some of the strength of iron in it, even as you saw iron mixed with clay. ...In the time of those kings, the God of heaven will set up a kingdom that will never be destroyed, nor will it be left to another people. It will crush all those kingdoms and bring them to an end, but it will itself endure forever. …The great God has shown the king what will take place in the future." (verses 31-45 NIV)

So, the dream showed the Babylonian ruler that other world powers would succeed his empire, and that the Kingdom of God would eventually replace them all.

Daniel's later prophecies used symbolic "beasts" to reveal who those successors would be. Nebuchadnezzar's Babylonian Empire would fall to the Medo-Persian Empire, followed later by the Greek Empire. ("The two-horned ram that you saw represents the kings of Media and Persia. The shaggy goat is the king of Greece." – Daniel 8:20-21 NIV) Here in chapter 2, Babylon was the image's head of gold, Persia the chest and arms of silver, and Greece the belly and thighs of bronze. Although Daniel did not name it (because it had not yet come into existence as a nation in his day), commentators are nearly unanimous in identifying the Roman Empire as the legs of iron.

But where is Left Behind's "Global Community" ruled by world Potentate Nicolae Carpathia? The only mention here of a government ruling "the whole world" is the reference to the "bronze" belly and thighs of the statue, the Greek empire of Alexander the Great. "After you [Babylon], another kingdom will rise, inferior to yours. Next, a third kingdom, one of bronze, that will rule over the whole earth." (Dan. 2: 39 NIV) What did Daniel mean by that expression? Evidently that Babylon and its Persian, Greek and Roman successors all ruled over the civilized world, the known world of their day, from the standpoint of the nation of Israel and the Jewish people. None of them ruled over southern Africa, east Asia, Australia or North and South America. Daniel was not speaking of what we today would call a 'world government.'

Nothing in Daniel chapter 2 speaks of the sort of global one-world government portrayed in the Left Behind novels. Although the authors of *Left Behind* may see a future world government "clearly predicted" there, it is not clear where they derive that understanding.

> And four great beasts came up from the sea, diverse
> from one another. (KJV)

"The beast" of Revelation is portrayed in the Left Behind novels as a
man named Nicolae Capathia. (See the discussion of Revelation chapter
13 later in this book.) But the beasts here in Daniel's prophecy form the
basis for the symbolism in Revelation, and they tell a different story.

The seventh chapter of Daniel deals with visions the prophet saw in a
dream. (verse 1) Four fearsome beasts appeared before him,
representing a series of "kings" or governments (verse 17) that would
rule over the world inhabited by Daniel's people, the Jews.

The footnote on verse 3 in *The New Scofield Reference Bible* says, "The
monarchy vision of Nebuchadnezzar (ch. 2) covers the same order of
fulfillment as Daniel's beast vision." Paralleling the four parts of the
statue in Daniel chapter 2, the "four great beasts" in chapter 7 verse 3 are
likewise the Babylonian, Persian, Greek and Roman empires. Bible
commentators have long agreed on this. Reformer John Calvin was
familiar with the works of other scholars and declared, "It is clear that
the four monarchies are here depicted. But it is not agreed upon among
all writers which monarchy is the last, and which the third. With regard to
the first, all agree in understanding the vision of the Chaldean Empire,
which was joined with the Assyrian, as we saw before. For Nineveh was
absorbed by the Chaldeans and Babylonians." (Calvin's *Commentaries on
the Book of Daniel*, volume 2) So, while there were differences in the
details, most traditional writers agreed Daniel was referring to the
Babylonian, Persian, Greek and Roman empires.

These beasts are the key to understanding the seven-headed beast that
appears in the thirteenth chapter of John's Apocalypse or Revelation.
While Daniel's vision uses a different beast to represent each of four
successive empires and their offshoots, John's later vision rolls the four
beasts into one. Daniel's beasts have a total of seven heads and ten
horns, while John sees a single beast with seven heads and ten horns.

"The first was like a lion" (Dan. 7:4)	1 head	0 horns
"a second, like a bear" (Dan. 7:5)	1 head	0 horns
"another, like a leopard" (Dan. 7:6)	4 heads	0 horns
"a fourth beast, dreadful" (Dan. 7:7)	1 head	10 horns
Totals for the beasts of Daniel ch. 7	7 heads	10 horns

compare

The beast of Revelation ch. 13	7 heads	10 horns

While each of the four beasts Daniel saw stood for a successive empire, the composite beast John saw incorporated into one body the whole series of biblical ruling powers down through history. John's beast carried all seven heads and all ten horns on one body.

Why, then, do the authors of *Left Behind* show 'the beast' to be Nicolae Carpathia, a man, a single individual—when Scripture speaks plainly of empires? This is just one more area where this fiction series departs from the clear meaning of Scripture and the understanding held by Bible readers over the centuries.

Daniel 7:8, 21, 25

A fourth beast . . . it had ten horns. While I was thinking about the horns, there before me was another horn, a little one, which came up among them; and three of the first horns were uprooted before it. This horn had eyes like the eyes of a man and a mouth that spoke boastfully. . . . As I watched, this horn was waging war against the saints and defeating them . . .He will speak against the Most High and oppress his saints and try to change the set times and the laws. The saints will be handed over to him for a time, times and half a time. (NIV)

In his *Commentary on Daniel* Reformer John Calvin applied much of this to pagan Rome and declared that "the Caesars became more and more stirred up to carry on war against the elect, and to oppress the Church." He identified the little horn with the powerful Caesars who ruled the empire. Referring back to Daniel in his commentary on Matthew 24:15-28, he noted that believers would find themselves "enduring tribulations through an uninterrupted succession of many ages. There is no small consolation also in the phrase, *half a time*, (Daniel 12:7) for though the *tribulations* be of long continuance, yet the Spirit shows that they will not be perpetual. And, indeed, he had formerly used this form of expression: The calamity of the Church shall last through *a time, times, and half a time*, (Daniel 7:25.)" (Calvin's *Commentary on a Harmony of the Evangelists*)

While some writers have agreed with Calvin's analysis, others have proposed different meanings. In fact, this passage has been given a wide range of interpretations. "The learned are not agreed concerning this anonymous beast," wrote Matthew Henry (1662 – 1714) in his *Commentary on the Whole Bible*. "Some make it to be the Roman empire, which, when it was in its glory, comprehended ten kingdoms, Italy, France, Spain, Germany, Britain, Sarmatia, Pannonia, Asia, Greece, and Egypt; and then the little horn which rose by the fall of three of the other horns (*v.* 8) they make to be the Turkish empire. Others make this fourth beast to be the kingdom of Syria ...and then the *little horn* is Antiochus Epiphanes..." Matthew Henry concluded, however, that "this prophecy has primary reference to the Syrian empire, and was intended for the encouragement of the Jews who suffered under Antiochus... But yet it has a further reference, and foretels [sic] the like persecuting power and rage of Rome heathen, and no less in Rome papal, against the Christian religion, that was in Antiochus against the pious Jews and their religion."

English scientist and mathematician Sir Isaac Newton (1643-1727), better known for his laws of motion and universal theory of gravitation than for his religious writings, said of the little horn, "This is the Church of Rome." (*Observations Upon the Prophecies of Daniel and the Apocalypse*, p. 76) Colonial American Congregationalist theologian and missionary Jonathan Edwards (1703-1758), who also served as president of Princeton, wrote, "the little horn is said to have a mouth speaking very great things, and his look to be more stout than his fellows. This also was verified in the pope, and the church of Rome." (*A History of the Work of Redemption*)

Left Behind departs from the traditional Protestant interpretations by moving the fulfillment of these verses to the future, during a supposed seven-year tribulation. The Antichrist Nicolae Carpathia appoints ten kings to rule the world under his supreme authority, but three of them rebel and must be crushed or "uprooted." The three horns uprooted are "the president of the United States . . . joined by the leaders of England and Egypt." (*Are We Living in the End Times?* p. 167) Authors LaHaye and Jenkins portray this in their second novel *Tribulation Force*: American president "Fitzhugh...was merely playing into Carpathia's hands. This was all part of the foretold future. The uprising against Antichrist would be crushed and would initiate World War III." (p. 424)

LaHaye and Jenkins assert that the verses above speak of the Antichrist (*Are We Living in the End Times?* page 274), and throughout their writings they assume that "the saints" mentioned here are "Tribulation saints" — men and women who come to faith in Christ during an end-times tribulation period. (The later novels in the Left Behind series show Antichrist Carpathia oppressing them during the three and a half years of the Great Tribulation.) Apparently they forget that the Old Testament writers used the term "saints" (Hebrew *kodesh* = 'holy' or 'set apart') to refer to the Jews. At Mount Sinai, according to Moses, God gave his law to the "saints." (Deut. 33:2) King David called true-worshipping Jews of his day "the saints who are on the earth." (Ps. 16:2 NKJV)

In this case the prophet Daniel was given visions of "what will happen to your people [the Jews] in the days to come" (Dan. 10:14 *Jerusalem Bible*), including "a time of distress such as has not happened from the beginning of nations until then" from which "your people [the Jews]...will be delivered." (Dan 12:1 NIV) So, when Daniel used the term "saints," he had in mind God's 'holy people'—Daniel's own people, the Jews.

The events Daniel foretold were to be in the future from his day, but that does not necessarily mean that they still lie in the future from our day. Has there already been an episode in history that could have fulfilled this prophecy? A time when the Jews were handed over for three and a half years to a boastful foreign ruler like the "little horn"?

The Bible book of Esther relates in great detail an attempt to exterminate the Jewish people during the reign of the Medo-Persian empire. Haman the Agagite persuaded king Ahasuerus "to destroy all the Jews" throughout the empire, which ruled "from India unto Ethiopia." (Esther 3:6, 8:9) The king was not aware that his own wife, Queen Esther, was a Jewess. She and her uncle Mordecai worked together to save their people. But Ahasuerus was not at all like Daniel's little horn. He did not oppress the Jews and was only tricked into decreeing their destruction. When he realized the truth, he came to their rescue. He did not actually wage war against the Jews. Haman was not like the little horn either, because he was not a national ruler—just an appointed official serving under the king.

If the Bible would record in such detail Haman's *failed* attempt to exterminate the Jews, is it logical to believe that Scripture would omit mention of Hitler's Holocaust that claimed some six million Jewish lives? Could that be the fulfillment of Daniel's words above?

Daniel wrote that his people would be handed over to a foreign ruler for "a time, times and half a time." It was a similar time span of three and a half years from when the first Nazi extermination camp became operational in December 1941 until the last death camp was liberated in May 1945. (Concentration camps set up to house Jews existed before this, but camps set up specifically to carry out genocide were operational for just three and a half years.) "Where was God?" people ask. "Why didn't God rescue his Chosen People?" Perhaps it was because this was the time Daniel foretold when his people would be handed over to a fierce enemy.

In *Armageddon: The Cosmic Battle of the Ages*, volume eleven in the Left Behind series, the authors show their Antichrist, Nicolae Carpathia, attempting to implement "the final solution of the Jewish problem." (p. 223) Unfortunately, that scenario had already played out during the rule of Adolph Hitler.

Hitler's Third Reich could certainly fit the description of the "little horn." It waged war against the Jewish people. (Daniel does not speak of them here as a "nation," but rather as a "people"—which would fit the circumstances of the Jews at the time of the Holocaust.) The Third Reich spoke boastfully against God like the little horn. And it was an offshoot of the Roman Empire that rose up after the other offshoot nations, the "ten horns" of Daniel chapter 7. France, Spain, England and other fragments of the former Roman empire had already been established as sovereign nations for centuries, when Germany finally united in the 1800's under Baron von Bismark. Like Daniel's little horn, Germany "came up among" the other ten as a late-comer.

As noted in some of the quotes above, many Christian commentators since the Reformation have identified the "little horn" as the papacy, which also rose as a secular power after the Roman Empire disintegrated into "ten horns." And they liken the oppressed "saints" to Christians persecuted by the Pope of Rome during the Inquisition. (Compare the discussion below of Revelation 11:3-5.) Daniel certainly had in mind his own people, the Jews, who are referred to as *saints* throughout the Old Testament, but we can't rule out a further application to Christians oppressed by the papacy. Prophecies can have both primary and secondary fulfillments.

In any case, if the prophet had lived to see the excesses of the Inquisition against Bible-believers, and had lived to see his own people gassed and cremated in extermination camps for a time and times and half a time, he would not have found a need for Left Behind's fictional scenario to fulfill his prophecy.

Daniel 9:24-27

> Seventy weeks are determined upon thy people and upon thy holy city, to finish the transgression, and to make an end of sins, and to make reconciliation for iniquity, and to bring in everlasting righteousness, and to seal up the vision and prophecy, and to anoint the most Holy. Know therefore and understand, that from the going forth of the commandment to restore and to build Jerusalem unto the Messiah the Prince shall be seven weeks, and threescore and two weeks: the street shall be built again, and the wall, even in troublous times. And after threescore and two weeks shall Messiah be cut off, but not for himself: and the people of the prince that shall come shall destroy the city and the sanctuary; and the end thereof shall be with a flood, and unto the end of the war desolations are determined. And he shall confirm the covenant with many for one week: and in the midst of the week he shall cause the sacrifice and the oblation to cease, and for the overspreading of abominations he shall make it desolate, even until the consummation, and that determined shall be poured upon the desolate. (KJV)

In their official defense of Left Behind theology titled *The Truth Behind Left Behind*, with Introduction by Tim LaHaye, apologists Mark

Hitchcock and Thomas Ice write that "The seven-year Tribulation is a cornerstone of the entire Left Behind series." (page 89) Then they go on to discuss Daniel 9:24-27 as the basis for this teaching, calling this passage "the indispensable key to all prophecy." (page 90)

But there is a problem with using this particular passage as a "key" to interpreting prophecy, and then deriving from it a seven-year Tribulation as a "cornerstone" for Left Behind theology. The problem is that the wording of the passage is confusing. What the words actually say is debatable, even before any attempt to understand what they mean. Sincere translators and experts on the original language have come up with wide variations in both wording and meaning. Is it sound practice to build an entire theological teaching on a "key" or "cornerstone" that is so uncertain?

For example, notice how the *New International Version* renders the same verses, with that translation's footnotes in parentheses to show alternative renderings:

> "Seventy 'sevens' (Or *weeks*; also in verses 25 and 26) are decreed for your people and your holy city to finish (Or *restrain*) transgression, to put an end to sin, to atone for wickedness, to bring in everlasting righteousness, to seal up vision and prophecy and to anoint the most holy. (Or *Most Holy Place*; or *most holy One*) Know and understand this: From the issuing of the decree (Or *word*) to restore and rebuild Jerusalem until the Anointed One (Or *an anointed one*; also in verse 26), the ruler, comes, there will be seven 'sevens,' and sixty-two 'sevens.' It will be rebuilt with streets and a trench, but in times of trouble. After the sixty-two 'sevens,' the Anointed One will be cut off and will have nothing. (Or *off and will have no one*; or *off, but not for himself*) The people of the ruler who will come will destroy the city and the sanctuary. The end will come like a flood: War will continue until the end, and desolations have been decreed. He will confirm a covenant with many for one 'seven.' (Or *week*) In the middle of the 'seven' (Or *week*) he will put an end to sacrifice and offering. And on a wing *of the temple* he will set up an abomination that causes desolation, until the end that is decreed is poured out on him (Or *it*)." (Or *And one who causes desolation will come upon the pinnacle of the abominable temple, until the end that is decreed is poured out on the desolated city*) (NIV, Revised Edition of 1983)

The phrase "of the temple" in the last sentence is not found in the original Hebrew, but is added by the NIV translators. Also in the last sentence the translators' alternative renderings indicate that the end may be poured out on *him* or on *it* or on the *city*—city being a word not found in the original, but added in an attempt to complete the meaning.

Moreover, a comparison with a number of other translations will reveal even more possible readings, besides those offered in the NIV footnotes.

In addition to all of these translation issues, there are also problems with understanding the grammar. There is disagreement as to whether the pronoun *he* in "He will confirm a covenant" refers to "the Anointed One" or to "the ruler who will come." These alternatives drastically affect the meaning.

We should recognize, of course, that God intentionally left certain portions of Scripture unclear or ambiguous, just as Christ spoke in parables on purpose. Some of Jesus' listeners walked away in disgust; some looked to the religious authorities of their day to put their own spin on Jesus' words; others went to the Lord privately to learn the meaning of what he said, or simply continued following him with full trust that he would make the meaning known in his own due time. Occasional obscurity in Scripture should not undermine our faith in God and his written Word, but it should make us cautious about seizing upon one of many competing human interpretations, and then using that questionable interpretation as the foundation for our faith.

In this case, it is important to recognize that this passage is one of the most obscure or puzzling sections of the entire Bible. Besides the debate over what it *means*, there is considerable controversy over what it actually *says* in the first place. The words themselves can be translated in different ways. Does it make sense to use this passage as the foundation for a whole system of belief? Yet that is exactly what Left Behind does.

Not only that, but the authors of Left Behind turn the traditional understanding of this passage on its head. For example, consider the phrase, "he shall confirm the covenant with many for one week ." As will be shown below, Reformers Martin Luther and John Calvin both understood the "he" who confirms the covenant to be Jesus Christ himself. Bible readers down through the centuries shared that understanding. The Left Behind series, however, teaches that "he" is the Antichrist, fictionalized in the novels as Nicolae Carpathia. What a dramatic reversal!

But there is much more revealing information here; let's look at this passage in its entirety.

The seventy weeks or seventy sevens are nearly universally understood by Christian commentators as referring to seventy seven-year periods, or a total of four hundred ninety years (70 x 7 = 490), applying the prophetic use of "a day for a year" found at Numbers 14:34 and Ezekiel 4:6.   This was naturally assumed to be a contiguous period of 490 consecutive years, until the 1800s when John Nelson Darby's teaching introduced the thought that there would be a parenthesis, or a gap of nearly 2000 years between the first 483 and the final 7 years. It is the final seven-year period that has been adopted by the Left Behind movement as the Tribulation. "In other words," Tim LaHaye and Jerry Jenkins write in *Are We Living in the End Times?*, "483 of the 490 years 'decreed' for Daniel's people have already elapsed; the divine 'counter' stopped just before the death of Jesus, with seven years still left to go. That remaining seven-year period is what we call the Tribulation." (p. 153)

But what basis is there to claim that the 490 years should be interrupted in this manner? Daniel certainly did not suggest any such gap. Nor is such a gap taught elsewhere in Scripture. Yet it is key to the thinking of the Left Behind authors. To use their own illustration, they suggest that God's prophetic clock has stopped ticking as long as the Church is upon the earth, and will resume ticking after Christians are raptured to heaven. Unfortunately, they offer no biblical basis for this assertion.

The traditional understanding is that the 490 years ran uninterrupted from beginning to end. The first 483 years brought us to the commencement of Jesus' ministry, and the final 7 years consisted of Christ's three-and-a-half year ministry plus another three-and-a-half years during which the Apostles preached the Gospel to the original Covenant people, the Jews. This is well stated by Martin Luther:

> "For when Christ sent out the Gospel through the ministry of himself and of the Apostles, it lasted three or three and a half years, that it almost amounts to the calculation of Daniel, namely the 490 years. Hence he also says, Christ shall take a half a week, in which the daily offerings shall cease; that is, the priesthood and reign of the Jews shall have an end; which all took place in the three and a half years in which Christ preached, and was almost completed in four years after Christ, in which the Gospel prospered the most, especially in Palestine through the Apostles (that when they opened their mouth, the Holy Ghost fell as it were, from heaven, as we see in the Acts of the Apostles), so that

a whole week, or seven years, established the covenant, as Daniel says; that is, the Gospel was preached to the Jews, of which we spoke before." (Martin Luther's "Sermon for the Twenty-Fifth Sunday after Trinity; Matthew 24:15-28" from his Church Postil, first published in 1525)

Calvin spoke similarly, emphasizing that the middle of the last 'week' occurred at the time of Christ's sacrificial death on the Cross:

> "The angel now continues his discourse concerning Christ by saying, *he should confirm the treaty with many for one week.* ...the angel says, *Christ should confirm the covenant for one week...*" (Lecture Fifty-First)

> "In the last Lecture we explained how *Christ confirmed the covenant with many during the last week...*" (Lecture Fifty-Second)

> "The Prophet now subjoins, *He will make to cease the sacrifice and offering for half a week.* We ought to refer this to the time of the resurrection. For while Christ passed through the period of his life on earth, he did not put an end to the sacrifices; but after he had offered himself up as a victim, then all the rites of the law came to a close. ...This is the Prophet's intention when he says, *Christ should cause the sacrifices to cease for half a week.* ...Christ really and effectually put an end to the sacrifices of the Law..." (Lecture Fifty-Second, *Commentary on Daniel - Volume 2* by John Calvin)

So, after the Babylonian exile of the Jews there are 69 weeks of years (483 years) from the command to rebuild Jerusalem, until the coming of God's Anointed One, the Messiah. Then there immediately follows a 70th week (7 years) of favor for God's covenant people, the Jews: Jesus' 3 1/2 year ministry exclusively to the Jews plus 3 1/2 years of the Apostles bringing Jews into the New Covenant (Jer. 31:31)— before opening the door to widespread Gentile conversion.

There is no biblical basis for abandoning this long-held understanding of Scripture to embrace the contrary teaching of Left Behind. And, since proponents of the new teaching see their interpretation of this passage as the *key* and the *cornerstone* of their belief, that entire Left Behind structure rests on very shaky ground.

Daniel 11:36-45

And the king shall do according to his will; and he shall exalt himself, and magnify himself above every god, and shall speak marvelous things against the God of gods, and shall prosper till the indignation be accomplished; for that which is determined shall be done. Neither shall he regard the gods of his fathers, nor the desire of women, nor regard any god; for he shall magnify himself above all. . . . And at the time of the end shall the king of the south push at him: and the king of the north shall come against him like a whirlwind, with chariots, and with horsemen, and with many ships; and he shall enter into the countries, and shall overflow and pass over. He shall enter also into the glorious land, and many countries shall be overthrown: but these shall escape out of his hand, even Edom, and Moab, and the chief of the children of Ammon. He shall stretch forth his hand also upon the countries: and the land of Egypt shall not escape. But he shall have power over the treasures of gold and of silver, and over all the precious things of Egypt: and the Libyans and the Ethiopians [shall be] at his steps. . . . And he shall plant the tabernacles of his palace between the seas in the glorious holy mountain; yet he shall come to his end, and none shall help him. (KJV)

Left Behind authors LaHaye and Jenkins claim that "the king of the north" in the latter part of Daniel chapter 11 is their post-Rapture Antichrist, Nicolae Carpathia. (*Are We Living in the End Times?* Pages 275-276) In this they follow the example of C.I. Scofield, whose notes assert that Daniel "overleaps the Church Age" in verse 36 when discussing the time of the end. "Here the discussion . . . which had to do with Palestine and the Jews up till the time of Antiochus Epiphanes . . . overleaps the Church Age and centuries to 'the time of the end.'" (Footnote on Daniel 11:36 in *The New Scofield Reference Bible*, 1967, Oxford University Press.) However, for readers whose thinking is not already colored by dispensationalist assumptions, there is no basis for Scofield's assertion that the Church is already raptured, and no basis for the assertion by LaHaye and Jenkins that Daniel is foretelling an individual like Nicolae.

Throughout his eleventh chapter, Daniel discusses "the king of the north" and "the king of the south." Scholars have traditionally agreed that both *kings* are actually *kingdoms*, not individuals. Scholars also generally agree that the chapter begins by predicting that the Persian domination Daniel lived under would be replaced by the Greek empire. Then, according to verse 4, the domain of Alexander the Great would be divided into four parts after his death. (This had already been foretold in Daniel 8:21-22.) Alexander's four generals, who inherited his kingdom, then wage war against each other. Daniel describes their rivalry from the perspective of the land of Israel and the Temple Mount, "the glorious land" (vs. 41) and "the holy mountain" (vs. 45), with one faction "north" of Israel fighting against the other faction "south" of Israel.

Over the centuries the king of the north and the king of the south change their identity—they are no longer Alexander's generals, but rather the kingdoms and empires that eventually succeed them centuries later in "the time of the end." Their identity at this point is no longer as certain as it was when following the immediate succession of heirs to Alexander the Great. Calvin acknowledged that commentators offered a wide variety of interpretations, but he concluded that the correct understanding is to see 'the king of the north' as the Roman Empire: "This passage is very obscure, and has consequently been explained in very opposite ways by interpreters. And whatever is obscure, is usually doubtful . . . The Jews, for instance, are not agreed among themselves . . . . The Christian expositors present much variety, but the greater number incline towards Antichrist as fulfilling the prophecy. . . . I apply it entirely to the Roman Empire." (*Commentaries on the Prophet Daniel*) By "Antichrist" Calvin meant, of course, the traditional understanding of this term among his contemporaries, rather than the dispensationalist or Left Behind view which was unknown in his day. Many of his contemporaries applied Daniel's words to the papacy, but Calvin himself saw fulfillment in the occupation of the Holy Land by the Roman Empire: "This language of the angel—they shall fix the tents of their palace—will suit the Romans exceedingly well, because they reigned there in tranquility after the east was subdued." (*Commentaries on the Book of the Prophet Daniel* by John Calvin)

As Calvin noted, however, there has been a lot of disagreement as to the identity of Daniel's king of the north and king of the south in the time of the end. Commentators have been far from unanimous.

Sir Isaac Newton commented to the effect that "these nations compose the Empire of the Turks, and therefore this Empire is here to be understood by the King of the North." (*The Prophecies of Daniel and The Apocalypse*, p. 189) That Islamic empire and its successors held the Holy Land until the Turks suffered defeat along with their German allies during the First World War and Jerusalem was taken from them by a British and Jewish force in 1917. The description of a king rejecting the gods of his fathers and the desire of women could fit Islam, which Luther and Calvin considered the Eastern 'horn' or 'leg' of the Antichrist. (See the discussion of 2 Thess. 2:4)

Or, viewed another way, the prophecy could fit the Nazi Third Reich, which considered itself to be the *third* incarnation of the Holy Roman Empire. (See the discussion of Daniel 7:8, 21, 25.)

In any case, there is nothing in this passage that would require a post-Rapture Antichrist like the Nicolae Carpathia character of the Left Behind series. Although traditional commentaries disagree among themselves as to *which* kingdom or empire is meant, they agree that Daniel referred to a such a world power, rather than to an individual like the fictional Carpathia.

Daniel 12:1

> . . . and there shall be a time of trouble, such as never was since there was a nation even to that same time; and at that time thy people shall be delivered, every one that shall be found written in the book. (KJV)

Jesus paraphrases this passage in Matthew 24:21-22 and Mark 13:19-20 when he speaks of "great tribulation, such as was not since the beginning of the world to this time, no, nor ever shall be." (Matt. 23:21 KJV) So, this is the Great Tribulation—which Left Behind portrays as the future world-wide reign of Nicolae Carpathia, the Antichrist. But did Daniel have in mind such a time of trouble for a world of people 'left behind' after the Rapture? No. The angel told him it was a time of trouble for "thy people," the Jews. And Jesus' words also show it to be the trouble that would come upon that people, the Jews, after their rejection of the Messiah. This is the way that Reformer John Calvin understood it. Commenting on the parallel passages in Matthew 24 and Luke 21, he wrote:

"21 *For there will then be great tribulation.* Luke says also, that there will be *days of vengeance, and of wrath on that people, that all things which are written may be fulfilled.* For since *the people,* through obstinate malice, had then broken the covenant of God, it was proper that alarming changes should take place, by which the earth itself and the air would be shaken. True, indeed, the most destructive plague inflicted on the Jews was, that the light of heavenly doctrine was extinguished among them, and that they were rejected by God; but they were compelled—as the great hardness of their hearts made it necessary that they should be compelled—to feel the evil of their rejection by sharp and severe chastisements.

. . . And therefore Christ says that, unless God put a period to those calamities, the Jews will utterly perish, so that not a single individual will be left; but that God will remember his gracious covenant, and will spare *his elect,*

. . . But a question arises, how was it on *account of the elect* that God set a limit to these calamities, so as not utterly to destroy the Jews, when many of those who were saved were reprobate and desperate? The reply is easy. A part of the nation was preserved, that out of them God might bring his *elect,* who were mixed with them, like the seed after the chaff has been blown off." (Calvin's *Commentary on a Harmony of the Evangelists*)

So, Calvin understood Daniel's "time of trouble" to refer to the calamities the Jews suffered, beginning shortly after they rejected the Messiah in the first century. There is no compelling reason to reject Calvin's wisdom, to adopt the contrary teaching of Left Behind.

Compare also our discussion of Matthew 24:21.

Joel 3:18

And it shall come to pass in that day, that the mountains shall drop down new wine, and the hills shall flow with milk. (KJV)

A major problem with the Left Behind books is the authors'

failure to apply sound principles of interpretation when it comes to distinguishing between literal and symbolic language in Scripture. In *Kingdom Come: The Final Victory*, characters living in Israel after the return of Christ walk to the Judean "foothills, where the streams had become pure white milk. Having only half finished his meal, Rayford knelt and cupped both hands in the white cascade." Some distance from the streams of milk there are also literal streams of red wine: "There, gushing down the mountainsides were deep purple channels, collecting in great, beautiful pools below." (page 13) One of the characters quotes Joel 3:18 to explain this phenomenon.

The problem is that the language in this Bible passage is clearly poetic, symbolizing a land that has become abundantly productive. Similar language is used throughout the books of Moses when speaking of the Promised Land; for example, compare Deuteronomy 26:9 which says, "He brought us to this place and gave us this land, a land flowing with milk and honey." When the Jews left Egypt and occupied the land of Canaan, did they encounter literal streams of milk and honey flowing down from the hills? No, of course not. Well, Joel 3:18 obviously uses the same sort of poetic symbolism. Left Behind authors LaHaye and Jenkins insult the reader's intelligence when they, in all seriousness, teach that white milk and red wine will literally gush from the hillsides.

Can this objection be dismissed with the excuse that the story is intended to be fictional, and not to be taken seriously? Perhaps, if that were the case—but it is not. A "Note from Dr. Tim LaHaye" at the end of the volume portraying streams of milk and wine says, "We've attempted to follow the Scriptures carefully in a time-honored pattern of taking the Bible literally wherever possible. . . . we believe what we have portrayed here will happen someday." (*Kingdom Come: The Final Victory*, pages 355-356)

Why would the Left Behind authors play fast and loose with biblical symbols like this—interpreting literally passages that are clearly symbolic? As will be show later, this sets a pattern that allows them to abandon the understanding Bible readers have had for centuries, and to apply new meanings to the prophecies of Daniel and the Revelation. (Compare the discussions of symbolism in Revelation 1:1, 9:1-9 and 9:16-19.)

Zechariah 12:2-3

I am going to make Jerusalem a cup that sends all the surrounding peoples reeling. Judah will be besieged as well as Jerusalem. On that day, when all the nations of the earth are gathered against her, I will make Jerusalem an immovable rock for all the nations. All who try to move it will injure themselves. (NIV)

In the twelfth Left Behind novel, *Glorious Appearing* (p. 276), authors Tim LaHaye and Jerry Jenkins portray the fulfillment of this passage as taking place during a battle with the Antichrist at the end of a seven-year tribulation. However, in *Are We Living in the End Times?* (pp. 46-47) they apply it more realistically to the world situation since 1967 when Jerusalem once again became the Jewish seat of government, after a gap of nearly two thousand years. In a series of wars from 1967 onward, Jerusalem has indeed sent the surrounding peoples reeling, despite numerous United Nations resolutions in which nearly all the nations of the earth have joined together against her. Will the nations also unite for future military action against Jerusalem? Time will tell. But, for such a scenario to occur, there is no need for a seven-year tribulation.

Zechariah 12:8-9

In that day shall the Lord defend the inhabitants of Jerusalem; and he that is feeble among them at that day shall be like David; and the house of David shall be like God, like the angel of the Lord before them. And it shall come to pass, in that day, that I will seek to destroy all the nations that come against Jerusalem. (KJV)

In the eleventh Left Behind novel, *Armageddon: The Cosmic Battle of the Ages*, LaHaye and Jenkins apply this passage to an attack on Jerusalem by the "Global Community" forces under their Antichrist, Nicolae Carpathia, at the end of their seven-year tribulation. (p. 328) However, the fictional scene that they paint bears little resemblance to the prophecy.

Zechariah says the Lord will defend the inhabitants of Jerusalem, but in the novels they are almost totally defeated, most of them killed, with only a few hold-outs defending a tiny patch of land on Temple Mount when God finally steps in. (Volume twelve, *Glorious Appearing: The End of Days*, pages 20, 110, 272) Hardly the victory Zechariah proclaims!

Also, while the prophet speaks of "all the nations that come against Jerusalem," the Left Behind novels have the attack take place years after the nations have surrendered their national sovereignty to a one-world government headed by Nicolae Carpathia. There are no longer any nations or national armies. The forces attacking Jerusalem are those of the Global Community—a single unified army under a single flag.

Zechariah's prophecy doesn't really fit the fictional world of the Left Behind novels at the end of their seven-year tribulation. Rather, it fits our world today, with many independent nations hostile to the state of Israel and demanding, through United Nations resolutions, that the Jews surrender their hold over Jerusalem. Will this hostility finally reach a point where God steps in to defend the city and "destroy all the nations that come against Jerusalem"? Time will tell. But there is nothing in Zechariah's words that would justify the interpretation presented in the Left Behind series.

Verse-by-Verse Answers—New Testament

Matthew 4:1-11

> Then Jesus was led by the Spirit into the desert to be tempted by the devil. After fasting forty days and forty nights, he was hungry. The tempter came to him and said, "If you are the Son of God, tell these stones to become bread." Jesus answered, "It is written: 'Man does not live on bread alone, but on every word that comes from the mouth of God.'" Then the devil took him to the holy city and had him stand on the highest point of the temple. "If you are the Son of God," he said, "throw yourself down. For it is written: " 'He will command his angels concerning you, and they will lift you up in their hands, so that you will not strike your foot against a stone.'" Jesus answered him, "It is also written: 'Do not put the Lord your God to the test.'" Again, the devil took him to a very high mountain and showed him all the kingdoms of the world and their splendor. "All this I will give you," he said, "if you will bow down and worship me." Jesus said to him, "Away from me, Satan! For it is written: 'Worship the Lord your God, and serve him only.'" Then the devil left him, and angels came and attended him. (NIV)

In a virtual paraphrase *The Rising: Before They Were Left Behind*, the first prequel to the Left Behind series, applies this entire passage to the Antichrist. We see Nicolae Carpathia as a young man whisked away from his bedroom in his silk pajamas and deposited in the wilderness by the devil, who tells him, "Wait here. I shall return for you in forty days." (p. 370)

Famished, filthy and emaciated at the end of that period, Nicolae greets the returning Satan by gladly accepting all of his invitations—turning stones into bread, throwing himself down from a pinnacle of the Temple, and accepting rulership over all of the kingdoms of the world in return for an act of worship—the very same temptations that Christ rejected. (pp. 376-379)

What basis is there for applying this passage to the Antichrist? None whatsoever in Scripture. But *The Rising* is, after all, just a novel. And novelists are granted a certain amount of poetic license, even when writing historical or futuristic fiction.

The problem, however, is that many readers gain their understanding of end times prophecy primarily from these novels. And many Left Behind enthusiasts regard these books almost as sacred volumes and put stock in what they say as the only valid exposition of the Word of God. For example, consider the reaction a dear Christian friend experienced when she told her eighty-year-old aunt, a lifelong church member and Bible reader, that she took issue with some of the Left Behind story. The elderly relative challenged her, "Well! If you don't want to believe the Bible!"

Consider also that there are now online communities modeled after the fictional Tribulation Force, the group set up by heroes Rayford Steele and Cameron ("Buck") Williams to battle the Antichrist. Search the web, and you will find online clubs and discussion groups whose members seem to see themselves as real-life counterparts of the fictional characters—sometimes even using "Tribulation Force" as part of their communal name.

In any case, because the Left Behind novels are taken seriously by many Christian readers and are more widely read than most non-fiction works on the topic, the authors bear some responsibility. *The Rising* depicts a genetically-engineered Antichrist fathered by two homosexuals and conceived at the behest of a Satan-worshiping organization—a far cry from anything found in Scripture. I feel it is in poor taste to apply this passage of Scripture to this fictional Antichrist, and thus trivialize the temptation of Christ.

Matthew 7:21-23

"Not everyone who says to me, 'Lord, Lord,' will enter the kingdom of heaven, but only he who does the will of my Father who is in heaven. Many will say to me on that day, 'Lord, Lord, did we not prophesy in your name, and in your name drive out demons and perform many miracles?' Then I will tell them plainly, 'I never knew you. Away from me, you evildoers!'" (NIV)

This is a passage of Scripture largely passed over and ignored by the Left Behind novels, and given little prominence in discussions by Left Behind apologists.   On page 73 of *Are We Living in the End Times?* LaHaye and Jenkins quote the last two verses and say merely, "I believe the church at large today is in the same plight as those religionists described by Jesus in Matthew 7:22-23."   But they ignore the fact that "that day" Christ spoke of is the day he returns, when some who claim him as Lord will "enter the kingdom," while "evildoers" who claim him as Lord will go to their punishment.

Their novels have Christ returning twice, so which return would fit Jesus' words about "that day"?   At the Lord's first return, according to their story, true believers are raptured but imitation Christians like those addressed here by Christ are merely left behind for a second chance. This would not fit "Depart from me, you evildoers!"—an expression that Jesus used to indicate final judgment. (See below.)   At Christ's second return, according to their fictional account, believers are all clearly marked in their foreheads with a holographic cross that only other believers can see, and unbelievers are marked visibly with a tattoo showing loyalty to the devil incarnate.   Everything is black and white; everyone is clearly marked as a follower of Christ or an enemy.   This doesn't fit the scenario Jesus described, either.

In the verses above Jesus shows himself returning to a world full of "many" imitation Christians—much like today's world, rather than that portrayed in *Armageddon* and *Glorious Appearing*, the two later novels in the Left Behind series.   The story presented in those books leaves no room for many pseudo-Christians to be unmasked at Christ's return.

Nor does the original *Left Behind* novel, the first in the series, allow for such a scenario.   Churches are largely emptied by the Rapture, leaving behind only a few stragglers who recognized themselves as pretenders. None of them protest their lot, or point to their supposed Christian works in self-justification.

In any case, Jesus' use of the expression "away from me, you evildoers" or "depart from me, ye that work iniquity" (KJV) indicates that those addressed are sent off to their eternal punishment.   Compare Matthew 25:41, "Depart from me, ye cursed, into everlasting fire."   Christ is not saying to them, 'Depart from me into a seven-year-long second chance.'

No, this passage in Matthew's Gospel makes plain that at Christ's return believers are rewarded and unbelievers' fate is sealed by their unbelief—even those who pretended to be Christians by attending Church and going through the motions. Sadly, this may include those who, as a result of reading *Left Behind*, adopted a wait-and-see attitude and put off making a decision for Christ in the expectation that they would have an extra seven years to make that choice.

Commenting on Matthew 7:21, Reformation leader John Calvin wrote that Christ "speaks not only of false prophets, who rush upon the flock to tear and devour, but of hirelings, who insinuate themselves, under fair appearances, as pastors, though they have no feeling of piety." (Calvin's *Commentary on a Harmony of the Evangelists*) Hypocritical assistant pastor Bruce Barnes in the Left Behind novels would fit the latter description. According to Calvin he would face eternal punishment, but *Left Behind* gives him a second chance.

Matthew 13:30, 36-43

"Let both grow together until the harvest. At that time I will tell the harvesters: First collect the weeds and tie them in bundles to be burned; then gather the wheat and bring it into my barn." ... Then he left the crowd and went into the house. His disciples came to him and said,"Explain to us the parable of the weeds in the field." He answered, "SThe one who sowed the good seed is the Son of Man. The field is the world, and the good seed stands for the sons of the kingdom. The weeds are the sons of the evil one, and the enemy who sows them is the devil. The harvest is the end of the age, and the harvesters are angels. As the weeds are pulled up and burned in the fire, so it will be at the end of the age. The Son of Man will send out his angels, and they will weed out of his kingdom everything that causes sin and all who do evil. They will throw them into the fiery furnace, where there will be weeping and gnashing of teeth. Then the righteous will shine like the sun in the kingdom of their Father. He who has ears, let him hear.'"
(NIV)

The Left Behind series makes little or no mention of this parable. But Jesus tells the story of "the man who sowed good seed in his field" in Matthew chapter 13, verses 24 through 30, and then gives the explanation in verses 36 through 43. Perhaps the Left Behind authors fail to refer to it because it does not fit their version of the end times.

According to Jesus the good seed and the weeds grow together down through history until "the end of the age," at which time the weeds are first thrown into the fire, and then after that, the wheat is gathered. But Left Behind presents it the other way around: first the gathering of wheat at the Rapture, and then the weeds tossed into the fire seven years later. This contradicts the order Jesus gives in the parable: "First collect the weeds and tie them in bundles to be burned; then gather the wheat."

In his notes on verse 30, C. I . Scofield says, "This will have its fulfillment at the end of the age (v. 40) when Christ returns to reign. The wicked will be destroyed. The Church, translated before the tribulation, will be gathered into the millennial kingdom . . ." (*The New Scofield Reference Bible*) So, he tries to get around the problem by having the wheat, although gathered first in his pre-tribulation rapture theory, set aside for seven years and not brought into the kingdom until after the weeds are disposed of—quite a stretch of the imagination.

Really, no matter which way you look at it, the parable of the wheat and the weeds does not allow for a seven-year tribulation at the end of the age. It doesn't fit the beginning of a seven-year period, because the weeds are not sent into everlasting punishment at that time, according to Left Behind. Nor does it fit the end of the seven years described in the Left Behind novels, where there is already a clear separation between those with the mark of the cross on their forehead and those wearing the mark of the beast. Jesus shows the wheat and the weeds growing "together" (vs. 30) throughout the history of the Church, until the harvesting angels finally do the separating and toss the weeds into the fire.

Compare, also, Jesus' parables of the sheep and the goats (See our discussion of Matt. 25:31-46.), the faithful and the evil slaves (See our discussion of Matt. 24:45-51.), and the wise and foolish virgins (See our discussion of Matt. 25:1-13.). All of them point to a sudden separation when Christ returns, with some rewarded and others sent into everlasting punishment at the same time, not seven years later.

> "Verily I say unto you, All these things shall come upon
> this generation." (KJV)

The Left Behind novels and their accompanying apologetic works make little or no mention of this verse—perhaps because it is a key to refuting their teachings concerning the Great Tribulation.

Dispensational futurists want to apply most or all of Matthew chapter 24, including its prediction of "great tribulation" (24:21), to a future "this generation" (24:34) during the end times, but they are forced to admit that Jesus applied exactly the same term—"this generation"—to his contemporary Jewish audience here in chapter 23. And both chapters form a continuous discourse. Matthew tells us Jesus spoke the words found in chapter 23, then "went out, and departed from the temple" (24:1) and spoke the words found in chapter 24. Is it reasonable to believe that Jesus would say "this generation" to refer to his contemporaries and then use the same term with a different meaning a few moments later?

Let's look more closely at chapter 23. What "things" are referred to here? And which "generation"? Jesus makes it unmistakably clear.

In Matthew chapter 23 Jesus was addressing the Pharisees. He called down "woes" upon them: "Woe unto you, scribes and Pharisees, hypocrites!" because they shut up the kingdom of heaven (vs. 13), because they devour widows' houses (vs. 14), because they make disciples for hell (vs. 15), because they elevate gold above the temple (vss. 16-22), because they engage in nit picking while neglecting the weightier matters of the law (vss. 23-24), and because they appear outwardly clean but are inwardly corrupt (vss. 25-33). He then reminded the Pharisees that they are "the sons of them who killed the prophets" and called them "ye generation of vipers." (vs. 31, 33) After foretelling that they would persecute and kill his disciples the same way their fathers killed the prophets, "that upon you may come all the righteous blood shed upon the earth, from the blood of righteous Abel unto the blood of Zechariah, son of Barachiah," Jesus concluded with the sentence above: "Verily I say unto you, All these things shall come upon this generation."

Clearly this was the generation that stood there in Jesus' presence, the generation he was addressing in person. The punishment for their hypocrisy and their wickedness would come upon that very generation. Just upon the scribes and Pharisees? No, in his next sentence Jesus went on to say, "Jerusalem, Jerusalem, thou that killest the prophets, and stonest them who are sent unto thee." The punishment would come upon those religious leaders and their city of Jerusalem in that very generation.

Jesus pronounced these words in or around 30 - 33 A.D., and the armies of the Roman empire brought the destruction Jesus predicted upon the city in 70 A.D., less than forty years later, within the lifetime of "this generation."

Even the dispensational futurist notes in the Scofield Reference Bible admit this. The footnote on Matthew 23:36 says, "Thus history runs. Judgment falls upon one generation for the sins of centuries. The prediction of v. 36 was fulfilled in the destruction of Jerusalem in A.D. 70." But then its footnote on 24:34 says that the word *generation* "could not here mean those alive at the time of Christ," but applies instead to a "future generation" at the end times. This contradictory reasoning shows the lengths to which dispensational futurists must go to try to make Scripture fit their theories.

Jesus' use of the term "this generation" in Matthew chapter 23 defines his use of the same term in chapter 24, and makes it likely that the Great Tribulation began upon the Jewish people back in the first century, and is not an end-times event yet to come.

Compare the discussion of Matthew 24:34.

Matthew 23:38

"Behold, your house is left unto you desolate." (KJV)

This verse is a key to understanding "the abomination of desolation" sixteen verses later. "Verily I say unto you, all these things shall come upon this generation. O Jerusalem, Jerusalem..." Jesus said. "Behold, your house is left unto you desolate." (Matt. 23:37-38) He was warning of the coming desolation of the Holy City and its temple. And he was still speaking of the same thing when he quoted Daniel about "the abomination of desolation" and the need for "them who are in Judea" to "flee into the mountains." (Matt. 24:15-16) All of this happened in 70 A.D., when the city and temple were desolated by Roman armies. There is no basis for claiming this refers, instead, to some future action by a character like Left Behind's Nicolae Carpathia.

See also the discussion of Matthew 24:15-16

Matthew 24:1-8

"Jesus left the temple and was walking away when his disciples came up to him to call his attention to its buildings. "Do you see all these things?" he asked. "I tell you the truth, not one stone here will be left on another; every one will be thrown down." As Jesus was sitting on the Mount of Olives, the disciples came to him privately. "Tell us," they said, "when will this happen, and what will be the sign of your coming and of the end of the age?" Jesus answered: "Watch out that no one deceives you. For many will come in my name, claiming, 'I am the Christ,' and will deceive many. You will hear of wars and rumors of wars, but see to it that you are not alarmed. Such things must happen, but the end is still to come. Nation will rise against nation, and kingdom against kingdom. There will be famines and earthquakes in various places. All these are the beginning of birth pains. Nation will rise against nation, and kingdom against kingdom. There will be famines and earthquakes in various places. All these are the beginning of birth pains." (NIV)

Nothing in this book is meant to diminish the urgency of the times in which we live. Bible readers everywhere recognize in world events the signs the Scriptures tell us to look for. Although *Newsweek* magazine has credited authors Tim LaHaye and Jerry Jenkins with being "The New Prophets of Revelation" (May 24, 2004 cover caption), they are far from being the first among their contemporaries to proclaim the approach of Christ's return. Nor do they themselves claim such a distinction. Due to the phenomenal success of their books, they have simply been the most prominent in making this public declaration.

But such prominence does not guarantee that the details of their proclamation are correct. There was a time back in the 1830's and 1840's when the general public associated Christ's return with the predictions of Baptist layman William Miller. He calculated that the Second Advent would take place in 1843 or 1844, and tens of thousands (some estimate as many as half a million) became his followers as "Millerites," a nationally-recognized religious movement that attracted considerable public interest. When the dates Miller set passed without incident, his large-scale movement fell apart. But diehard believers remained to form the core of various "adventist" churches, from which eventually sprang the Advent Christian Church, the Seventh-day Adventist Church and the Jehovah's Witness organization—today embracing tens of millions of adherents. Each of these groups has its own scenario of how end times events can be expected to unfold.

Time will tell whose interpretation of the Bible's end times prophecies turns out to be correct—or whether the Lord surprises us with an unfolding of events that no one expected. The Apostle Paul wrote concerning some dubious preachers in his day, "What then? notwithstanding, every way, whether in pretence, or in truth, Christ is preached; and I therein do rejoice, yea, and will rejoice." (Philippians 1:18 KJV) Something similar can be said about modern efforts to interpret end times prophecy. Even those efforts that are based on faulty understanding of the precise details have contributed toward public anticipation of the grand event of Christ's return.

Much of the confusion stems from the fact that the disciples' question to Jesus in Matthew 24:3 involved three different things: the temple's destruction, Christ's coming and the world's end. The authors of Left Behind fail to properly sort out these three elements in Jesus' answer. A more traditional Protestant approach can be found in the writings of Methodist founder John Wesley. He sorted it out this way:

> "The disciples inquire confusedly, 1. Concerning the time of the destruction of the temple; 2. Concerning the signs of Christ's coming, and of the end of the world, as if they imagined these two were the same thing. Our Lord answers distinctly concerning 1. The destruction of the temple and city, with the signs preceding, ver. 4, &c., 15, &c. 2. His own coming, and the end of the world, with the signs thereof, ver. 29-31. 3. The time of the destruction of the temple, ver. 32, &c. 4. The time of the end of the world, ver. 36."

> - John Wesley's *Notes on the Bible*, Matt. 24:3

> "So when you see standing in the holy place 'the abomination that causes desolation,' spoken of through the prophet Daniel—let the reader understand—then let those who are in Judea flee to the mountains." (NIV)

According to the authors of the Left Behind series, "Both Daniel and John place this awful event in the middle of the Tribulation." (*Are We Living in the End Times?* page 123) But it would be more accurate to say that the event is placed there by LaHaye and Jenkins, not by Daniel and John. It is these fiction writers who say that this passage applies to a temple that will be rebuilt in Jerusalem in the future, and that the Antichrist will then desecrate that temple by slaughtering a pig and by erecting his own statue to be worshiped there. (*Desecration: The Antichrist Takes the Throne*, pp. 161-163)

A closer examination of Jesus' own words places "the abomination that causes desolation" in the first century, when the Romans entered the existing temple and subsequently desolated it and the city of Jerusalem.

The immediate context should make this clear. Just a few verses before mentioning "the abomination that causes desolation," Matthew records that Jesus said, "Jerusalem, Jerusalem, . . . Look, your house is left to you desolate." (Matt. 23:38 NIV) That same "house" or temple would be left *desolate* by something that causes *desolation* —the abomination that causes desolation.

Two verses later, at Matthew 24:1, we read that "Jesus left the temple" and the disciples called "his attention to its buildings." In the next verse, Jesus tells them about "these things" that "not one stone here will be left on another; every one will be thrown down." (vs. 2) In verse 3 the disciples ask, when will "this" happen? And thirteen verses later Jesus explains that the desolation will be accomplished by "the abomination that causes desolation." (vs. 15) Where, then, in this compact discussion, did Jesus switch from speaking about the temple he and his disciples were looking at, to bring up what would happen to a different temple in the distant future? Nowhere! The reasonable conclusion that any reader would normally reach is that the same temple forms the subject of the discussion throughout these seventeen verses. It is the same temple that is left "desolate" and faces "desolation."

Writing initially for a Jewish audience familiar with the Hebrew Scriptures, Matthew included Jesus' words quoting the prophet Daniel. Luke, on the other hand, captured words that would be more understandable to his Greek-speaking audience. In Luke's parallel account we read that Jesus said, "When you see Jerusalem surrounded by armies, you will know that its desolation is near. Then let those who are in Judea flee to the mountains." (Luke 21:20-21 NIV) What did Jesus say would be the signal for his first-century followers and others in Judea to flee to the mountains? That signal was "armies" surrounding the city according to Luke's account, and "the abomination that causes desolation" according to Matthew's account. Since both Gospel writers were relating the same warning message, and the same signal to flee the city, "the abomination that causes desolation" must be the Roman forces that later desolated the temple and the city.

How then can the Left Behind theologians come up with their interpretation that the Jewish temple will be rebuilt in modern times and that the abomination is a man named Nicolae Carpathia who "commits the ultimate blasphemy by appearing in the temple to declare that he is God" during the midst of a seven-year tribulation? (*Are We Living in the End Times?* Page 123) Only by presenting a very complex series of arguments. It is not a conclusion that unindoctrinated readers come to on their own when reading the Bible alone.

As mentioned earlier, there is some confusion, though, because the disciples added to their question about the Temple's destruction, "and what shall be the sign of your coming, and of the end of the world?" (Matt. 24:3 KJV) Although Jesus knew, of course, that these three events—the Temple's destruction, his second coming, and the end of the world—would not be simultaneous, he went on to answer their three questions together. So, it becomes necessary to discern which parts of Jesus' response refer to the first century devastation on Jerusalem, and which parts apply to his coming and the end of the world.

Martin Luther explained that Matthew "cooks both into one soup":

> In this chapter there is a description of the end of two kingdoms; of the kingdom of the Jews, and also of the kingdom of the world. But the two Evangelists, Matthew and Mark, unite the two—and do not follow the order as Luke did, for they have nothing more in view than to relate and give the words of Christ, and are not concerned about what was said either before or after. But Luke takes special pains to write clearly and in the true order,

and relates this discourse twice; first briefly in the 19th chapter, where he speaks of the destruction of the Jews at Jerusalem; afterwards in the 21st chapter he speaks of both, one following the other. Notice therefore that Matthew unites the two and at the same time conceives the end, both of the Jewish nation and of the world. He therefore cooks both into one soup. But if you want to understand it, you must separate and put each by itself, that which really treats of the Jews, and that which relates to the whole world.

(Martin Luther's "Sermon for the Twenty-Fifth Sunday after Trinity; Matthew 24:15-28" from his Church Postil, first published in 1525)

Commentators offer many opinions on how the various elements of Matthew Chapter 24 should be divided and grouped together. But such forensic reconstruction is not needed, if we follow Luther's advice. We need only compare Luke's account to gain a better understanding of what Jesus meant.

For century after century Bible readers knew that the two references were the same, and understood that "the abomination that causes desolation" had something to do with the armies of Imperial Rome that desolated the city of Jerusalem, together with its temple, in 70 A.D.

How did the Romans go beyond merely causing "desolation"? Why did they also deserve being labeled as an "abomination"? At the time of the Protestant Reformation Martin Luther wrote, "But the abomination of which Daniel writes is that the Emperor Cajus, as history tells, had put his image in the temple at Jerusalem as an idol, for the people to worship, after everything there had been destroyed." (Martin Luther's "Sermon for the Twenty-Fifth Sunday after Trinity; Matthew 24:15-28" from his Church Postil, first published in 1525)

John Wesley (1703-1791), father of the Methodist churches, wrote"When ye see the abomination of desolation—Daniel's term is, The abomination that maketh desolate, Dan. xi, 31; that is, the standards of the desolating legions, on which they bear the abominable images of their idols: Standing in the holy place—Not only the temple and the mountain on which it stood, but the whole city of Jerusalem, and several furlongs of land round about it, were accounted holy; particularly the mount on which our Lord now sat, and on which the Roman [sic] afterward planted their ensigns." (John Wesley's *Notes on the Bible*, Matt. 24:15)

So, the Roman forces were an *abomination* by virtue of their idolatrous images, and they caused *desolation* by desolating Jerusalem and its temple. Similar teaching prevailed in Protestant churches for hundreds of years, until the early 1900s when the Scofield Reference Bible popularized John Nelson Darby's concept of a seven-year tribulation and transported these events from the context of the Roman destruction of the Temple to a rebuilt third temple some time in the future.

See also the discussion of 1 Corinthians 3:16-17 and 2 Thessalonians 2:4.

Matthew 24:21

> "For then shall be great tribulation, such as was not since the beginning of the world to this time, no, nor ever shall be." (KJV)

Readers of the Left Behind series are taught that the great tribulation is a specific time period of three-and-a-half years that begins when antichrist Nicolae Carpathia, Potentate of the Global Community, sits down in a rebuilt Jewish temple in Jerusalem and declares himself to be God. (Compare *Are We Living in the End Times?* Page 123) Is that really what Jesus meant?

When Jesus told his disciples that the temple they had just visited in Jerusalem would be destroyed, they asked, "When will these things be? And what shall be the sign of your coming, and of the end of the world?" (Matt. 24:3 KJV) As part of his answer, Jesus spoke the words above. Did he mean that the "great tribulation" would occur in connection with the temple's destruction by the Romans in 70 A.D., or at the end of the world?

The context in Matthew's Gospel certain seems to indicate that the term "great tribulation" describes the Jewish people's suffering that would begin with the Roman attack:

> Then let them which be in Judaea flee into the mountains:
>
> Let him which is on the housetop not come down to take any thing out of his house:

Neither let him which is in the field return back to take his clothes.

And woe unto them that are with child, and to them that give suck in those days!

But pray ye that your flight be not in the winter, neither on the sabbath day:

For then shall be great tribulation, such as was not since the beginning of the world to this time, no, nor ever shall be.

And except those days should be shortened, there should no flesh be saved: but for the elect's sake those days shall be shortened.

(Matthew 24:16-22 KJV)

Yes, fleeing as refugees, without time to take any of their possessions with them, would certainly qualify as 'great tribulation' for the Jews.

Mark's Gospel quotes essentially the same words from Jesus' sermon as Matthew does, but Luke presents additional words.

Then let them which are in Judea flee to the mountains; and let them which are in the midst of it depart out; and let not them that are in the countries enter thereinto. For these be the days of vengeance, that all things which are written may be fulfilled. But woe unto them that are with child, and to them that give suck, in those days! for there shall be great distress in the land, and wrath upon this people. And they shall fall by the edge of the sword, and shall be led away captive into all nations: and Jerusalem shall be trodden down of the Gentiles, until the times of the Gentiles be fulfilled.

(Luke 21:21-24 KJV)

What Matthew calls "great tribulation" Luke calls "great distress in the land, and wrath upon this people." It is clearly a time of suffering for the Jews, "this people," rather than an end-times post-rapture tribulation on the entire world, as presented in the Left Behind series. In his *Commentary on a Harmony of the Evangelists, Matthew, Mark and Luke* Calvin draws the same obvious conclusion from the parallel between Matthew's account and Luke's:

"21 *For there will then be great tribulation.* Luke says also, that there will be *days of vengeance, and of wrath on that people, that all things which are written may be fulfilled.* For since *the people,* through obstinate malice, had then broken the covenant of God, it was proper that alarming changes should take place, by which the earth itself and the air would be shaken. True, indeed, the most destructive plague inflicted on the Jews was, that the light of heavenly doctrine was extinguished among them . . .

(See above the discussion of Daniel 12:1, where Calvin's commentary is quoted at greater length. He applies the *great tribulation* to the sufferings that came upon the Jewish people, beginning in the first century, after their rejection of the Messiah.)

Besides making it clear that it is a tribulation on the Jewish people, Luke's account also sheds light on its duration. Matthew mentioned merely that it would be "shortened," actually the Greek word KOLOBOO, which Vine's *Expository Dictionary of New Testament Words* indicates means "cut off, amputate...curtail." So it is shortened in the sense of being abruptly halted, rather than in the sense of being a short period as opposed to a long period. But Luke includes the details that the Jews would be "led away captive into all the nations" and that Jerusalem would remain in Gentile hands until "the times of the Gentiles" are fulfilled. The Jews remained scattered among all the nations until their return to the Promised Land, which culminated in the establishment of the modern state of Israel in 1948, and they regained control over Jerusalem during the Six-Day War in 1967.

Writing in the late 1800s, Albert Barnes could not have known of these more recent events, but he wrote this on the subject: "Verse 21. *There shall be great tribulation.* The word tribulation means *calamity*, or *suffering*. Lu 21:24 has specified in what this tribulation should consist. 'They shall fall by the edge of the sword, and shall be led away captive into all nations; and Jerusalem shall be trodden down of the Gentiles, until the times of the Gentiles shall be fulfilled.' That is, until the time allotted for the Gentiles to do it shall be fully accomplished; or as long as God is pleased to suffer them to do it." (*Notes on the New Testament*, Matthew 24:21)

If the great tribulation on the Jews can be seen as spanning the entire time period of their foreign dispersion—from the destruction of Jerusalem until the founding of modern Israel—then it must have climaxed in the Holocaust of 1941-1945. With some six million Jews killed in the gas chambers and death camps of Nazi-controlled Europe, and with its stated purpose being the 'Final Solution of the Jewish problem' by exterminating the race, this tribulation would surely fit Jesus' description: unless those days were cut short, no flesh would have been saved. The Jews would have been wiped out, had it not been cut short or stopped.

Nothing in Jesus' description of this "great tribulation" allows for taking it out of its Jewish context and applying it instead to the post-rapture world at large.

See also the discussion of Daniel 12:1.

Matthew 24:27

> "For as the lightning cometh out of the east, and shineth even unto the west; so shall also the coming of the Son of man be." (KJV)

Jesus makes it plain that his return will be an unmistakable event. It will be like a super-bright lightning blast that illuminates the sky from one horizon to the other. You can't miss it.

Left Behind theology, on the other hand, calls for a secret coming of the Son of man at the rapture, and then another coming seven years later at the end of a tribulation period. Authors LaHaye and Jenkins call this "Two Phases to Christ's Second Coming," rather than a second coming followed by a third coming. Their nonfiction works feature elaborate charts and tables listing the Bible verses that speak of Christ's return, and separating these verses into two groups: those supposedly referring to the first invisible second coming at the rapture, and those alleged to refer to the second phase of the second coming, otherwise called Christ's "glorious appearing." (See, for example, *Are We Living in the End Times*, pages 99-100.)

Having written several books on Jehovah's Witnesses, I find this two-phase second coming a familiar concept. The Adventist splinter group that Watchtower founder Charles Taze Russell fellowshipped with before breaking off to form his own religion expected Christ to return in the year 1874. Although nothing notable occurred on the chosen date, the die-hard members of the sect refused to accept that their chronology had been in error; instead, they decided Jesus must have returned invisibly. His glorious appearing to judge this wicked world would come a few years later. JWs have since moved the date of Christ's supposed invisible return to 1914—no problem, since the date depends on complex explanations rather than anything that people actually witnessed. They expect Christ to come again a second time to destroy the wicked very soon.

The problem with both interpretations—that of Jehovah's Witnesses and the similar two-phased second coming of the Left Behind movement—is that both depend on fancy arguments rather than on the plain reading of Scripture. Folks who sit down by the fireplace and read only their Bible don't come up with either interpretation. You have to read the Watchtower books or the Left Behind books to conclude anything other than what the angel said: "This same Jesus, who has been taken from you into heaven, will come back in the same way you have seen him go into heaven." (Acts 1:11 NIV)

And, when Christ does return, it will be like a flash of lightning that no one will miss.

Matthew 24:29

> "Immediately after the tribulation of those days shall the sun be darkened, and the moon shall not give her light, and the stars shall fall from heaven, and the powers of the heavens shall be shaken." (KJV)

Here the authors of *Left Behind* series encounter problems with their claim to interpret Bible prophecy "literally." (Compare page 4 of *Are We Living in the End Times* by LaHaye and Jenkins.) In the closing novels of the series they do indeed portray the sun and moon darkened, but they cannot show the stars literally falling from heaven, since the stars are mammoth heavenly bodies immensely larger than the earth. The earth could literally fall onto the surface of a star, sooner than stars could actually fall to the earth. The novels settle, instead, for chunks of rock falling from the sky and producing streaks of light that we today call meteors or "shooting stars." This similarity in the English language, however, offers no real basis to claim that Jesus was talking about such falling pieces of stone. Nor are the novels able to picture the powers of the heavens literally "shaken."

The very size relationship between earth and stars mandates that the language Jesus uses here must be figurative. Then his words fit perfectly the view that the "tribulation" here refers to the centuries-long suffering of the Jews beginning with the Roman destruction of Jerusalem, climaxing in the Holocaust, and ending with the re-establishment of the state of Israel. (See the discussions of Dan. 12:1 and Matt. 24:21.) It was immediately after that tribulation that the heavens lost their power as men began to rocket into outer space. The heavenly bodies figuratively fell from the sky, as they came within mankind's reach through manned space flight.

While the Jews were returning to the Promised Land after their tribulation, the scientists who had worked on Adolph Hitler's V-1 and V-2 rockets began working for the victorious allied powers. Soon test pilots flew experimental jets above earth's atmosphere for the first time in human history. Soviet Russia put its Sputnik satellite into orbit in 1957, followed shortly by the first manned space flights. Humans circled the moon, taking pictures of its dark side, and landed there to plant an American flag on this heavenly body. Truly, the powers of the heavens have been shaken.

A more traditional view was expressed by Calvin, who took "the tribulation of those days" to refer to the centuries-long sufferings of the Church:

> "Christ comes now to speak of the full manifestation of his kingdom, about which he was at first interrogated by the disciples, and promises that, after they have been tried by so many distressing events, the redemption will arrive in due time. . . . the Church shall have passed through the whole course of its *tribulations*. . . . *The tribulation of those days* is improperly interpreted by some commentators to mean the destruction of Jerusalem; for, on the contrary, it is a general recapitulation . . . of all the evils of which Christ had previously spoken. To encourage his followers to patience, he employs this argument, that the *tribulations* will at length have a happy and joyful result. As if he had said, 'So long as the Church shall continue its pilgrimage in the world, there will be dark and cloudy weather; but as soon as an end shall have been put to those distresses, a day will arrive when the majesty of the Church shall be illustriously displayed.' In what manner *the sun will be darkened* we cannot now conjecture, but the event will show. He does not indeed mean that *the stars* will actually fall, but according to the apprehension of men; and accordingly Luke only

predicts that *there will be signs in the sun, and in the moon, and in the stars.* The meaning therefore is, that there will be such a violent commotion of the firmament of heaven, that *the stars* themselves will be supposed to fall." (Calvin's *Commentary* on Matthew 24:29 and the parallel passages in Mark and Luke)

Calvin's explanation certainly fits both the Scriptures and the facts of history—the history of the Church and its tribulations.

Regardless of whether Jesus actually meant the tribulation upon the Jews or the tribulations the Church has passed though over the centuries, this passage offers no basis for postulating a future seven-year tribulation after the Church is taken to heaven.

Matthew 24:34

> "Verily I say unto you, This generation shall not pass, till all these things be fulfilled." (KJV)

What generation did Jesus mean by "this generation"?

Many writers have tried to identify it with a particular generation in modern times. Watchtower founder Charles Taze Russell identified it with "the 'generation' from 1878 to 1914." (*Studies in the Scriptures*, vol. 4, 1908 edition, page 605) His successors in the Jehovah's Witnesses leadership changed it to "the generation that saw the events of 1914." (*Awake!* magazine, October 22, 1995, page 4). *Left Behind* authors LaHaye and Jenkins say, "we believe 'this generation' refers to those alive in 1948. It may, however, mean those alive in 1967 or those alive in some yet future war when the Jews will once again gain total control of their holy city." (*Are We Living in the End Times?* page 59)

The context provides the best indication of which generation Jesus really meant. A few verses earlier he invoked a series of 'woes' upon the "teachers of the law and Pharisees" (Matt. 23: 13, 15, 16, 23, 25, 27, 29) and then told them, "upon you will come all the righteous blood that has been shed on earth, from the blood of righteous Abel to the blood of Zechariah son of Berekiah, whom you murdered between the temple and the altar." (Matt. 23:35) In the next verse he added, "I tell you the truth, all this will come upon this generation." (Matt. 23:36) And then he generalized this beyond just the Jewish religious leaders, to include their city: "O Jerusalem, Jerusalem..." (Matt. 23:37) All of this did indeed come upon that generation of Jews when Jerusalem was besieged by the Romans in 66 A.D. and desolated by them in 70 A.D.

Could Jesus reasonably be talking about a different generation just a few verses further on, at Matthew 24:34? No, because right after saying the above, "Jesus left the temple and was walking away" when he told his disciples, "not one stone here will be left on another; every one will be thrown down." (Matt. 24:1-2) Their question, "when will this happen" (vs. 3) led to Jesus' response which included again the same time factor, "this generation."

What has led so many commentators to try to apply the prophecy to a future generation, such as that of 1914, 1948 or 1967? As Martin Luther wrote, the disciples combined their question about when the temple would be destroyed with another question about when Christ would return, and Jesus answered both, which Matthew then "cooks both into one soup" in his account. (See Luther's full quote in our discussion of Matt. 24:15-16, above.) Matthew chapters 24 and 25 include both the timing of Jerusalem's destruction and references to Christ's return. But the biblical context makes it clear that "this generation" applies specifically to the Jews in Jesus' audience who lived to see their city and temple desolated.

Yes, the dates 1948 (when the state of Israel was restored) and 1967 (when Jews took control of Jerusalem again after nearly two thousand years of Gentile control) are significant milestones in history and in the fulfillment of Bible prophecy, but there is no biblical basis for the authors of *Left Behind* to claim, as they do, that "'this generation' refers to" people alive in 1948 or 1967. (*Are We Living in the End Times?* page 59)

Compare the discussion of Matthew 23:36.

Matthew 24:37-42

"But as the days of Noah were, so shall the coming of the Son of man be. For as in the days that were before the flood they were eating and drinking, marrying and giving in marriage, until the day that Noah entered into the ark, and knew not until the flood came, and took them all away, so shall also the coming of the Son of man be. Then shall two be in the field; the one shall be taken, and the other left. ...Watch, therefore; for ye know not what hour your Lord doth come." (KJV)

Ever since Jesus gave this admonition, Christians have been watching for his coming. He said it would be like the days of Noah. God's favored people were saved in the Ark, and the disobedient were destroyed by the flood—at the same time. The Lord said his coming would be like that. He did not indicate that believers would be taken up in the rapture seven years prior to the destruction of the wicked, as *Left Behind* teaches; no, these events would happen at the same time, just as in the days of Noah.

From another angle, though, the modern reader can easily be confused when reading the verses above. Some writers argue strongly for the view that it is the righteous who are left behind. The use of the words *take* and *taken* can cause this misunderstanding, because they are tenses of the same word in English, but entirely different words are used here in Greek. Depending on the translation, the reader can get the impression that it is the wicked who are "taken" at the time of Christ's return, and that believers are "left." In the King James Version it says of Noah's wicked contemporaries, that "the flood came, and *took* them all away," and when Christ returns, "the one shall be *taken* and the other left." So, some think Jesus' words above mean that the wicked would be *taken* and his faithful followers would be *left*. While recently surfing Amazon.com's online bookstore, I counted four books with the title *I Want To Be Left Behind*.

However, this confusion is based largely on the English translator's choice of words, rather than on what the Gospel writer originally wrote. Whereas the King James Version and some other translations use forms of the same word *take* in both places, the original Greek uses different words with different meanings.

When Jesus said the flood "took them all away," it is the Greek word *AIRO* that is used of the fate of the wicked, and any Greek lexicon shows that it is translated *took . . . away*, rather than simply *took*. The flood "*took* them all *away*." For those "taken" when Christ returns, an entirely different word is used. It is *PARALAMBANO* and means *take* in the sense of *receive*. In another passage Jesus assured disciples, "I will come again, and receive (*PARALAMBANO*) you unto myself." (John

14:3 KJV) So, in Matthew 24:39 *AIRO* means "took" in the sense that the flood *took away* or *swept away* the wicked as some other translations render it, whereas the believers in verse 40 are *taken* in the sense of being *received* by Christ at the Rapture. So there is no basis for teaching, as some do, that the righteous are to be left behind.

For more about how the Left Behind novels misuse this passage, see the discussion of the parallel account in Luke 17:34-36; also, the discussion of Genesis 7:7-21 earlier in this book.

Matthew 24:44

> "Therefore be ye also ready: for in such an hour as ye think not the Son of man cometh." (KJV)

This verse sets the stage for the parables that follow immediately in Matthew 24:45 through 25:46, so it is a key to understanding each of those parables, which Jesus used to illustrate that he "will come at an hour when you do not expect him." (NIV) (These are the parables of the faithful and wise servant, the talents, the ten virgins, and the sheep and the goats.) Do the authors of *Left Behind* see verse 44 as applying to Christ's return at the Rapture, or to his supposed second return seven years later? This is an important question. Tim LaHaye and Jerry Jenkins answer it directly on page 116 of *Are We Living in the End Times?* They quote the verse and say, "Only the pre-Tribulation rapture preserves that at-any-moment expectation of His coming." So, they apply it to the rapture *before* the seven-year tribulation.

However, they don't go on from there to discuss in that book the parables Jesus used to illustrate this same point. Why not? Perhaps because the parables don't fit their story of those 'left behind' receiving a second chance. Each one of the parables shows faithful followers rewarded, and those who are found unfaithful thrown into "eternal punishment . . . where there will be weeping and gnashing of teeth" at the same time. (Matt. 24:46, 51 NIV) Instead, *Left Behind* shows the unfaithful given a second chance over the next seven years.

Keep Matthew 24:44 and its timing in mind as you read the discussions that follow, which consider each of these parables individually.

"Who then is the faithful and wise servant, whom the master has put in charge of the servants in his household to give them their food at the proper time? It will be good for that servant whose master finds him doing so when he returns. I tell you the truth, he will put him in charge of all his possessions. But suppose that servant is wicked and says to himself, 'My master is staying away a long time,' and he then begins to beat his fellow servants and to eat and drink with drunkards. The master of that servant will come on a day when he does not expect him and at an hour he is not aware of. He will cut him to pieces and assign him a place with the hypocrites, where there will be weeping and gnashing of teeth." (NIV)

This parable does not fit the end times scenario Left Behind presents, and therefore argues against the fictional seven-year tribulation having any basis in fact. How so? Well, the master returns and rewards the faithful and wise servant, while *at the same time* sending the unfaithful servant into everlasting punishment ("weeping and gnashing of teeth"). This could not describe an invisible return of Christ to rapture believers while leaving the rest behind to face seven years of tribulation, because no one is sent into everlasting punishment in this scenario.

Nor could it describe Left Behind's supposed second return of Christ, when all believers will display a holographic cross on their foreheads and unbelievers will wear the mark of the beast. The novels depict all of Christ's servants knowing that his Glorious Appearing is due precisely at the end of the seven years, rather than 'on a day when they do not expect him.' The novels also fail to depict any unfaithful servants of Christ who are found carrying on badly at his supposed second return.

So, the two-stage return of Christ presented in the Left Behind novels completely ignores this parable where Jesus shows the Master returning unexpectedly with eternal rewards and punishments for his faithful and unfaithful servants.

Bible-believing Christians have traditionally understood this parable to picture Christ and the Church at his return. Methodist founder John Wesley wrote, "If ministers are the persons here primarily intended, there is a peculiar propriety in the expression. For no hypocrisy can be baser, than to call ourselves ministers of Christ, while we are the slaves of avarice, ambition, or sensuality. Wherever such are found, may God reform them by his grace, or disarm them of that power and influence, which they continually abuse to his dishonour, and to their own aggravated damnation!" (John Wesley's *Notes on the Bible*, Matt. 24:51) So, Wesley expected Christ's return to plunge unfaithful clergymen into damnation, like the servant in Jesus' parable. Instead, Left Behind shows hypocritical assistant pastor Bruce Barnes receiving a second chance.

Compare, also, Jesus' parables of the wheat and the tares (See the discussion of Matt. 13:36-43.), the sheep and the goats (See the discussion of Matt. 25:31-46.), and the ten virgins (Matt. 25:1-13.). All of them point to a sudden separation when Christ returns, with some rewarded and others sent into everlasting punishment at the same time, not seven years later.

Matthew 25:1-13

"At that time the kingdom of heaven will be like ten virgins who took their lamps and went out to meet the bridegroom. Five of them were foolish and five were wise. The foolish ones took their lamps but did not take any oil with them. The wise, however, took oil in jars along with their lamps. The bridegroom was a long time in coming, and they all became drowsy and fell asleep. At midnight the cry rang out: 'Here's the bridegroom! Come out to meet him!' Then all the virgins woke up and trimmed their lamps. The foolish ones said to the wise, 'Give us some of your oil; our lamps are going out.' 'No,' they replied, 'there may not be enough for both us and you. Instead, go to those who sell oil and buy some for yourselves.' But while they were on their way to buy the oil, the bridegroom arrived. The virgins who were ready went in with him to the wedding banquet. And the door was shut. Later the others also came. 'Sir! Sir!' they said. 'Open the door for us!' But he replied, 'I tell you the truth, I don't know you.' Therefore keep watch, because you do not know the day or the hour." (NIV)

This parable belies the Left Behind theory that nominal Christians who fail to keep watch will have a second chance to enter the kingdom. Consider the novels' prominent character Bruce Barnes, the assistant pastor who finds himself left behind at the Rapture. He is certainly a 'foolish virgin' who failed to 'keep watch,' and was not ready when the bridegroom arrived and took the rest of his congregation to heaven. But, unlike those in the parable who find the 'door shut' because they had not kept watch, Bruce and others like him get a "Second Chance"—the title of the second volume of the Left Behind "Kids" series.

Such a thought is foreign to the understanding Bible readers have had for centuries. In the mid-1500's John Calvin (1509-1564) wrote, "all who shall not be ready at the very moment when they shall be called will be shut out from entering into heaven." (Calvin's *Commentary on a Harmony of the Evangelists*) The idea of a second chance at Christ's return was unknown to the Reformers. Two hundred years later in the early 1700's commentator Matthew Henry got the same point from Jesus' illustration: "The state of saints and sinners will then be unalterably fixed, and those that are shut out then, will be shut out forever." (*Matthew Henry's Commentary*, Vol. V, p. 371) And in the late 1800's British pastor and teacher Charles Haddon Spurgeon wrote, "when once in the last days as Master of the house he shall rise up and shut the door, it will be in vain for mere professors to knock, and cry Lord, Lord open unto us, for that same door which shuts in the wise virgins will shut out the foolish for ever." (*Morning and Evening: Daily Readings*, for the morning of June 5, titled "The Lord shut him in," commenting on Genesis 7:16). Yes, Bible readers have always understood that the 'foolish virgins' would not get a second chance.

Compare, also, Jesus' parables of the wheat and the tares (See the discussion of Matt. 13:36-43.), the sheep and the goats (See the discussion of Matt. 25:31-46.), and the faithful and the evil slave (See the discussion of Matt. 24:45-51). All of them point to a sudden separation when Christ returns, with some rewarded and others sent into everlasting punishment at the same time, not seven years later.

Matthew 25:14-15, 19

"For the kingdom of heaven is like a man traveling into a

far country, who called his own servants, and delivered unto them his goods. And unto one he gave five talents, to another two, and to another one, to every man according to his ability; and straightway took his journey. ...After a long time the Lord of those servants cometh, and reckoned with them." (KJV)

This is another of the parables Jesus used to illustrate his coming. As noted above, the authors of Left Behind say that the *unexpected coming* Jesus referred to is the Rapture before the seven-year tribulation. (See our discussion of Matthew 24:44.) But when the Lord of the servants comes in this parable, he rewards his faithful servants and casts "the unprofitable servant into outer darkness" where "there shall be weeping and gnashing of teeth." (vs. 30) Hypocritical assistant pastor Bruce Barnes in the Left Behind novels would certainly fit the picture of the unfaithful servant who failed to do business with his talent. But, instead of being thrown into outer darkness, he is given a second chance.

Writing later in *Glorious Appearing: The End of Days*, the Left Behind authors say it is at the *end* of the seven-year tribulation that some are "cast into outer darkness." (page 382) Yet Christ's appearing at that time is not portrayed as unexpected. These contradictory interpretations are a natural consequence of their attempt to divide the return of Christ into two separate events seven years apart.

Compare the discussions of the other parables at the end of Matthew chapter 24 and in Matthew chapter 25.

Matthew 25:31-46

"When the Son of Man comes in his glory, and all the angels with him, he will sit on his throne in heavenly glory. All the nations will be gathered before him, and he will separate the people one from another as a shepherd separates the sheep from the goats. He will put the sheep on his right and the goats on his left. ... Then the King will say to those on his right, 'Come, you who are blessed by my Father; take your inheritance, the kingdom prepared for you since the creation of the world. ... Then he will say to those on his left, 'Depart from me, you who are cursed, into the eternal fire prepared for the devil and his angels. ... Then they will go away to eternal punishment, but the righteous to eternal life." (NIV)

This parable offers strong evidence against the dispensationalist view of the rapture followed by a seven-year tribulation.

Here the Lord separates the sheep from the goats, those who treated him and his followers well from those who abused him by abusing his followers, and tells the abusers to "Depart from me... into everlasting fire" (vs. 41) Dispensationalists can't place this event at the rapture, because no one is sent into everlasting fire then, according to their theory. So, they must place it at the end of their seven-year tribulation.

However, the parable doesn't fit that situation either. Those who are sent into everlasting fire are surprised, and ask, "Lord, when did we see you hungry or thirsty or a stranger or needing clothes or sick or in prison, and did not help you?" (vs. 44) And even those rewarded ask, "'Lord, when did we see you hungry and feed you, or thirsty and give you something to drink?" (vs. 37) How unlike the picture the dispensationalists offer where, at the end of the seven years, nearly everyone is clearly marked with a cross on their forehead or the mark of the beast! No room for surprises in that case! Everyone is already clearly identified as being on Jesus' side or against him.

This "sheep-and-goats judgment" is discussed and portrayed in No. 12 of the Left Behind series, *Glorious Appearing: The End of Days*. It is shown to take place at the end of the seven years. One of the characters remarks, "Those are the 'goats' over there, the followers of Antichrist." (page 376) Apparently the authors forgot how they interpreted Matthew 24:44 above, stating that it applies to the Rapture, *before* the seven years. In that verse Jesus exhorted followers to be "ready" for his unexpected return and gave a string of parables illustrating this: the faithful and unfaithful servants, the ten virgins, the talents, and the sheep and goats. As noted above, on page 116 of *Are We Living in the End Times?* LaHaye and Jenkins quote verse 44 and say, "Only the pre-Tribulation rapture preserves that at-any-moment expectation of His coming." Here, though, they try to make the sheep and goats parable fit a later time. Such confusion should be expected—it is a natural consequence of trying to divide Christ's return into two different events.

It should also be noted that LaHaye and Jenkins apply Jesus' words, "whatever you did for one of the least of these brothers of mine" to the

Jews. (Matt. 25:40 NIV) They assert, "Those who honored the Jews are the sheep, and those who did not are the goats." (*Glorious Appearing*, pages 367-368) Was Jesus referring to the Jews as his "brothers" here? No, because the Lord made clear that "Whoever does the will of my Father in heaven is my brother." (Matt. 12:50) And Hebrews 2:11 explains that "those who are made holy" are the ones Jesus calls "brothers." So, Jesus was referring here to his faithful followers rather than to the Jews.

Mark 1:12-13

At once the Spirit sent him out into the desert, and he was in the desert forty days, being tempted by Satan. He was with the wild animals, and angels attended him. (NIV)

The Rising: Before They Were Left Behind has young Nicolae Carpathia (the future Antichrist) tempted by the devil after forty days in the wilderness, just like Christ. In the novels, the child Nicolae is conceived and raised by spirit mediums, and "the Spirit" that sends him into the desert is the evil spirit that they all channel and obey. Yet the passage above speaks of the temptation of Christ. There is nothing in Scripture to indicate any future application to a character like Carpathia. See the discussion of Matthew 4:1-11..

Mark 13:14-19

"But when ye shall see the abomination of desolation, spoken of by Daniel, the prophet, standing where it ought not (let him that readeth understand), then let them that be in Judea flee to the mountains. ... For in those days shall be affliction, such as was not from the beginning of creation which God created unto this time, neither shall be." (KJV)

It is instructive to compare this passage with the parallel accounts of Matthew and Luke. Where Matthew quotes Jesus briefly as foretelling "great tribulation" (24:21) Mark here reports, "in those days shall be affliction." Luke gives the most detail: "For these are days of vengeance . . . For there shall be great distress in the land, and wrath upon this people. They shall fall by the edge of the sword, and shall be led away captive into all nations, and Jerusalem shall be trodden down by the Gentiles, until the times of the Gentiles be fulfilled." (Luke 21:22-24) The "great tribulation" that Left Behind moves into the end times actually refers to the suffering of Jews that began with a Roman attack in ancient Judea.

Please see the discussion of related passages in Matthew above and in Luke below.

Luke 4:1-13

"Jesus, full of the Holy Spirit, returned from the Jordan and was led by the Spirit in the desert, where for forty days he was tempted by the devil. He ate nothing during those days, and at the end of them he was hungry. The devil said to him, "If you are the Son of God, tell this stone to become bread." Jesus answered, "It is written: 'Man does not live on bread alone.'" The devil led him up to a high place and showed him in an instant all the kingdoms of the world. And he said to him, "I will give you all their authority and splendor, for it has been given to me, and I can give it to anyone I want to. So if you worship me, it will all be yours." Jesus answered, "It is written: 'Worship the Lord your God and serve him only.'" The devil led him to Jerusalem and had him stand on the highest point of the temple. "If you are the Son of God," he said, "throw yourself down from here. For it is written: '"He will command his angels concerning you to guard you carefully; they will lift you up in their hands, so that you will not strike your foot against a stone.'" Jesus answered, "It says: 'Do not put the Lord your God to the test.'" When the devil had finished all this tempting, he left him until an opportune time." (NIV)

The Left Behind prequel, *The Rising*, applies these verses to its character Nicolae Carpathia. This supposed Antichrist is dropped off in the wilderness by the evil spirit mentoring him, where he goes without food and water for forty days. When the devil reappears, Carpathia accepts the offer of world rulership. This is a pure flight of fancy, since there is nothing in Scripture to indicate such an application.

See also the discussion of Matthew 4:1-11 in this book.

Luke 17:34-36

> I tell you, in that night there shall be two men in one bed; the one shall be taken, and the other shall be left. Two women shall be grinding together; the one shall be taken, and the other left. Two men shall be in the field; the one shall be taken, and the other left. (KJV)

According to noted religious commentator John Dart, writing in *Christian Century* magazine, "The 'Left Behind' fiction series by Tim LaHaye and Jerry Jenkins borrows its title from passages like those in Luke 17 in which Jesus describes events of the end times. Verses 34 and 35 are widely interpreted to mean that those taken are the lucky ones. Moreover, Left Behind fans and others influenced by dispensationalist theology tend to see the ones taken as 'raptured' heavenward to be with the Lord." (September 25-October 8, 2002 p. 9, available online at http://www.religion-online.org/showarticle.asp?title=2601)

Yes, when read in the context of dispensationalist theology this passage may seem to suggest a world of people 'left behind' by the Rapture to face a seven-year tribulation. But, is there any basis for that interpretation when the passage is read in its original context in the Bible itself? No. The dispensationalists take it out of context. Jesus added relevant information in the words he spoke just before and right after the words quoted above. Let's read the passage in this context:

Then he said to his disciples, "The time is coming when you will long to see one of the days of the Son of Man, but you will not see it. Men will tell you, 'There he is!' or 'Here he is!' Do not go running off after them. For the Son of Man in his day will be like the lightning, which flashes and lights up the sky from one end to the other. But first he must suffer many things and be rejected by this generation.

"Just as it was in the days of Noah, so also will it be in the days of the Son of Man. People were eating, drinking, marrying and being given in marriage up to the day Noah entered the ark. Then the flood came and destroyed them all.

"It was the same in the days of Lot. People were eating and drinking, buying and selling, planting and building. But the day Lot left Sodom, fire and sulfur rained down from heaven and destroyed them all.

"It will be just like this on the day the Son of Man is revealed. On that day no one who is on the roof of his house, with his goods inside, should go down to get them. Likewise, no one in the field should go back for anything. Remember Lot's wife! Whoever tries to keep his life will lose it, and whoever loses his life will preserve it. I tell you, on that night two people will be in one bed; one will be taken and the other left. Two women will be grinding grain together; one will be taken and the other left."

"Where, Lord?" they asked. He replied, "Where there is a dead body, there the vultures will gather."

— Luke 17:22-37 (NIV)

The verses that precede the reference to 'one person taken and the other left' are very instructive. Jesus describes his future return as being similar to the days of Noah when those left behind outside the ark were destroyed, and the days of Lot when those left behind in Sodom were destroyed. So, when the context that precedes it is taken into consideration, this passage can hardly be used to teach that those left behind at Christ's return would be left alive for seven years.

What about the context that follows the verses in question? In the very next verse, the disciples asked the most obvious question about those who were to be left behind: "'Where, Lord?'" they asked. He replied, 'Where there is a dead body, there the vultures will gather.'" (Luke 17:37 NIV) So, Jesus indicated those left behind would be "dead" — with the vultures consuming their dead bodies. How does anyone get from this that they would be 'left behind' with seven years of life ahead of them? Only by ignoring the context.

In all fairness, it should be noted that proponents argue that the "body" in Luke 17:37 refers to the Church or Christian congregation as the body of Christ, and that the vultures are eagles, as in some translations. But there is nothing in the passage itself to indicate that Jesus resorted here to such mixing of metaphors. In fact, the only metaphorical use of the word "body" by the Lord was when he referred to the loaf of bread at the Last Supper as "my body." The Apostles years later referred to the Church as the body of Christ, but Jesus himself did not use the word "body" in that way in the Gospels.

Rather, Jesus portrayal of those left behind as dead bodies serving as food for birds perfectly parallels a passage in the Apocalypse that describes the same event. Revelation 19:7-21 tells of believers being taken to the wedding supper of the Lamb while those excluded (or left behind) serve as food for birds: "...all the fowls that fly in the midst of heaven, Come and gather yourselves unto the supper of the great God; That ye may eat the flesh of kings, and the flesh of captains, and the flesh of mighty men...and the flesh of all men, both free and bond, small and great...and all the fowls were filled with their flesh." (vss. 17-21)

So, a plain reading of Luke 17:34-36 in its full context leads to no other conclusion than that those left behind at the Flood, at the rain of fire and brimstone on Sodom, and at the return of Christ are all destroyed. If those left behind were to remain alive for seven years, the return of Christ would no longer be "like" the Flood and the destruction of Sodom. Jesus said his return would be like those earlier acts of God in which everyone left behind was left dead.

See also the discussion of the parallel passage at Matthew 24:37-42.

Luke 21:24

"They will fall by the sword and will be taken as prisoners to all the nations. Jerusalem will be trampled on by the Gentiles until the times of the Gentiles are fulfilled." (NIV)

According to Left Behind authors LaHaye and Jenkins the times of the Gentiles "will continue to the end of the Tribulation and the coming of Christ." (*Are We Living in the End Times?* p. 53) But Jesus said Jerusalem would "be trampled on by the Gentiles until the times of the Gentiles are fulfilled." History makes clear that this trampling ended in 1967, when the Jews captured the city and took control over it during the Six Day War. Gentiles no longer trample on Jerusalem, and have not done so since that decisive war. So, "the times of the Gentiles" must have ended.

In fact, comparison of Luke's words and their context with the parallel passages in Matthew's account sheds light on the Tribulation itself. While the Gentiles were having their "times" to trample freely on Jerusalem, the Jews were having their Tribulation. Their Holy City was trampled by the Romans in 70 A.D., a million Jews fell "by the sword" and the remainder were "taken as prisoners to all the nations." This was the beginning of a tribulation that lasted for centuries, climaxed in the Holocaust with six million more Jews killed, and ended when the state of Israel was restored and finally took Jerusalem back from the Gentiles.

See also the discussions of Mark 13:14-19 and Matthew 24:21.

John 14:2-3

> "In my Father's house are many rooms; if it were not so, I would have told you. I am going there to prepare a place for you. And if I go and prepare a place for you, **I will come back and take you to be with me** that you also may be where I am." (NIV)

Yes, the Rapture is a true biblical doctrine, but not the *secret* Rapture as portrayed in Left Behind. It is alluded to here, and described in greater detail in 1 Thessalonians 4:17. There is no need to take issue with the fact that *Left Behind* describes a time when believers are caught away to be with the Lord. We might take issue with the way the first novel in the series shows all the world's children raptured—the babies of believers and unbelievers alike. And we might take issue with the way the fifth novel *Apollyon* shows the pope raptured (page 53), the pope who Luther, Calvin and the other Reformers identified as the Antichrist. But I will leave those arguments to another writer. The main problem addressed in this book is that the novels teach that those who reject Christ get a 'second chance' for another seven years after Christ takes the Church home to be with him.

Acts 1:11

> "This same Jesus, who has been taken from you into heaven, will come back in the same way you have seen him go into heaven." (NIV)

Jesus went to heaven visibly; the disciples had just *seen* him go into heaven. Would he come back in a secret rapture—invisibly? No, the angel said "this same Jesus" will "come back in the same way you have seen him go into heaven."

The entire Left Behind series, however, is built on the premise that this verse does not mean what it says. The novels present Christ as returning invisibly at the Rapture, differently from the way the disciples had seen him go. The verse says, though, that he will return "in the same way."

In *The Remnant*, the tenth novel in the series, fictional Bible teacher Tsion Ben-Judah looks back from a time some four years following the Rapture and declares that Jesus "came back" and will yet again be "coming one last time." "Messiah was born in human flesh. He came again. And he is coming one more time." (pages 229, 233) When Christ supposedly "came back" nobody on earth saw him; he was invisible. Those who were left behind developed numerous theories as to what had happened, because nobody saw Jesus.

A number of sects have taught that Christ would return invisibly. The Jehovah's Witnesses have long held to the belief that Christ returned invisibly in the year 1914. Originally, however, they taught that the second coming occurred in 1874—a date they borrowed from an Adventist splinter group Watch Tower founder Charles Taze Russell had associated with as a young man. Certain Adventists had anticipated a visible return of Christ in 1874 but, when nothing happened, they gladly embraced the invisible-return theory. (See my book *Jehovah's Witnesses Answered Subject by Subject*, pages 19-27 and 183-186.)

Such sects typically depend on the authority of their leader to attach meanings to Bible verses that go beyond or even contradict the plain meaning of the text to an unprejudiced reader. A similar group dynamic takes place when Christians who view *Left Behind* authors Tim LaHaye and Jerry Jenkins as "The New Prophets of Revelation" (cover of *Newsweek* magazine, May 24, 2004) allow their convoluted arguments to explain away Acts 1:11, or to attach a meaning to the text that is contrary to what it plainly says. In their desire to make everything fit the dispensational scheme of things, they are forced to interpret such verses, rather than accept them at face value.

However, Christ's return "in the same way" the apostles "saw" him go to heaven precludes any teaching of an invisible return.

1 Corinthians 3:16-17

"Know ye not that ye are the temple of God, and that the Spirit of God dwelleth in you? If any man defile the temple of God, him shall God destroy; for the temple of God is holy, which temple ye are." (KJV)

The seven-year tribulation that is the centerpiece of Left Behind theology depends on the theory that the Jewish temple will be rebuilt in Jerusalem, that Old Testament animal sacrifices will again be offered at that temple, and that the Antichrist will put an end to those sacrificial offerings at the mid-point of the seven years. "That there will be a third temple is predicted by the prophet Daniel, the apostles Paul and John, and none other than the Lord Jesus Himself. They all taught that Israel's third temple will be rebuilt." (*Are We Living in the End Times?* by LaHaye and Jenkins, p. 122) All of this, however, ignores a basic teaching of the New Testament, namely, that God no longer dwells in a temple made of stones, but rather in the great spiritual temple, which is the Church, the Christian congregation.

Addressing "Jerusalem, Jerusalem, thou that killest the prophets, and stonest them who are sent unto thee," Jesus went on to tell the Jews, "Behold, your house is left unto you desolate." (Matt. 23:37-38 KJV) The *New English Bible* renders this last phrase, "there is your temple, forsaken by God." After the Jewish people climaxed their rebellion by rejecting, not only the prophets, but also the very Son of God, the God of Israel no longer had any use for their temple or their priesthood.

Martin Luther understood that it was the spiritual temple that the Antichrist would deal with, rather than a rebuilt Jewish temple in Jerusalem. He expressed it this way in one of his sermons:

"St. Paul prophesied all this, when in 2 Thess. 2, 3-4, he calls him: "The man of sin and the son of perdition, he that opposeth and exalteth himself against all that is called God or that is worshipped; so that he sitteth in the temple of God, setting himself forth as God."

But that the Papists want to turn this passage from themselves and say: Christ and Paul are speaking of the temple of Jerusalem, that Antichrist shall sit and rule there, amounts to nothing. For Christ says here, that Jerusalem together with the temple shall have an end, and after its destruction it shall never be rebuilt. Therefore since Paul is pointing to the time after the Jewish kingdom, and the destruction of the material temple, it cannot be understood otherwise than of the new spiritual temple, which as he says himself, we are." (Martin Luther's "Sermon for the Twenty-Fifth Sunday after Trinity; Matthew 24:15-28" from his *Church Postil*, first published in 1525)

The Jerusalem temple and its priesthood had served their purpose, since they were merely shadows pointing to the eventual real High Priest, Jesus Christ, and the ultimate sacrifice of the Lamb of God. "But Christ being come an high priest of good things to come, by a greater and more perfect tabernacle, not made with hands, that is to say, not of this building." (Heb. 9:11 KJV) A rebuilt Jerusalem temple would, therefore, have no part in God's purpose—except in the fictional Left Behind series. Bible readers who believe what the Apostle Paul wrote to the Corinthians realize that God's temple in the end times is the Christian Church, not a stone building that some expect to be rebuilt in Jerusalem.

See also the discussion of 2 Thessalonians 2:4.

1 Corinthians 15:50-53

"I declare to you, brothers, that flesh and blood cannot inherit the kingdom of God, nor does the perishable inherit the imperishable. Listen, I tell you a mystery: We will not all sleep, but we will all be changed—in a flash, in the twinkling of an eye, at the last trumpet. For the trumpet will sound, the dead will be raised imperishable, and we will be changed. For the perishable must clothe itself with the imperishable, and the mortal with immortality." (NIV)

In *The Truth Behind LEFT BEHIND* with Introduction by Tim LaHaye, authors Mark Hitchcock and Thomas Ice declare this to be a 'key passage' on the Rapture (p. 24). And so it is. The Rapture is plainly taught in Scripture. As a critic of the Left Behind series, I have no quarrel with their teaching that Christ will return to rapture the Church.

The problem is that they add to this a number of nonbiblical twists.

The first of these is the idea that it will be a *secret* rapture, that Christ remains invisible and unseen throughout the process of returning, raising dead believers back to life, and rapturing the Church. The second distortion is the notion that Jesus comes back *twice*—seven years apart. And the third is the belief that the Rapture is followed by a seven-year tribulation offering a second chance for unbelievers.

To refute these notions, please see the discussions of Matthew 7:21-23, 24:21, 24:27 and Acts 1:1 in this book.

1 Thessalonians 1:10

"Jesus who delivers us from the wrath to come." (RSV)

Authors LaHaye and Jenkins present this verse as one of the reasons "why the Rapture must be pre-Tribulation." "The church is to be delivered from the wrath to come." (*Are We Living in the End Times*, pp. 107, 110) In their view the "wrath to come" is a seven-year tribulation, and Christ delivers Christians by rapturing them just before the tribulation begins.

However, it is a stretch to claim that delivering the Church from God's wrath requires removing the Church from the earth. In the Lord's prayer Jesus taught us to pray, "deliver us from evil." Does this mean we are asking to be raptured from the earth before anything evil befalls us? No, the context indicates the prayer refers to daily temptations and every-day evils, just as it refers to ordinary "daily bread." (Matthew 6:11-13 KJV) Christ delivers us from evil without removing us from the scene. Likewise, he can deliver Christians from God's final wrath without removing Christians from the earth.

Psalm 91 tells how God will "deliver" the faithful. "Because he hath set his love upon me, therefore will I deliver him. He shall call upon me, and I will answer him. I will be with him in trouble; I will deliver him." (Ps. 91:14-15 KJV) The Psalm speaks of warfare, pestilence and destruction on a grand scale, but does not imply that the believer would have to be removed from the scene in order to be delivered from such wrath. Rather, the promise to the believer is that God will "cover thee...under his wings." (vs. 4) "A thousand shall fall at thy side, and ten thousand at they right hand, but it shall not come near to thee. Only with thine eyes shalt thou behold and see the reward of the wicked." (vs. 7-8)

In a similar manner, Jesus could deliver us from the wrath to come by shielding us as that wrath descends all around us. Of course, he may choose to rapture us before the wrath begins. But, in any case, 1 Thessalonians 1:10 certainly does not prove that there will be a secret Rapture followed by a seven-year tribulation.

Compare 1 Thessalonians 5:9 and the discussion of that verse.

1 Thessalonians 4:16-5:3

> "...we who are alive and remain until the coming of the Lord will by no means precede those who are asleep. For the Lord Himself will descend from heaven with a shout, with the voice of an archangel, and with the trumpet of God. And the dead in Christ will rise first. Then we who are alive and remain shall be caught up together with them in the clouds to meet the Lord in the air. And thus we shall always be with the Lord. Therefore comfort one another with these words. But concerning the times and the seasons, brethren, you have no need that I should write to you. For you yourselves know perfectly that the day of the Lord so comes as a thief in the night. For when they say, 'Peace and safety!' then sudden destruction comes upon them, as labor pains upon a pregnant woman. And they shall not escape." (NKJV)

The Apostle Paul wrote the above as one complete thought, even though it spans two chapters in our modern Bibles. (There were no chapter divisions in Paul's letters as found in the oldest manuscripts; it was later scribes who divided the passage above into chapters and verses.) Paul here says that Christ will descend, dead Christians will rise, living Christians will be raptured, and unbelievers will be taken by surprise and suddenly destroyed. Supporters of *Left Behind* don't like to read this complete passage in context.

Why not? Because a key element of Left Behind theology is the belief that Christ will return twice: first secretly at the Rapture, and then a second time openly, seven years later at the Glorious Appearing. The Apostle Paul embarrasses them by putting the Rapture and the destruction of the wicked together in one passage, above.

Apologists for *Left Behind* evidently recognize that unindoctrinated readers of the Bible would never come to the conclusion, on their own, that Christ returns twice, so they argue for their complex interpretation by arranging Scripture passages in charts and tables, with verses they attach to the Rapture under one heading and verses they believe are fulfilled seven years later under another heading. Thus Mark Hitchcock and Thomas Ice list 1 Thessalonians 4:13-18 under the "Rapture" heading in a series of charts on pages 36-38 of their book *The Truth Behind Left Behind*. Strangely, though, they don't include the verses that immediately follow in 1 Thessalonians 5:1-3. In fact, they don't refer to these verses at all in these charts—because the conclusion would be obvious: that Paul did *not* separate the Rapture from the execution of judgment on the wicked. Paul presented Christ as returning once to accomplish both purposes at the same time, as his inspired words above show in their full context.

1 Thessalonians 5:9

"For God hath not appointed us to wrath, but to obtain salvation by our Lord Jesus Christ" (KJV)

The authors of the Left Behind series consider this verse to be proof that the Rapture must occur before a seven-year Tribulation. They argue, "Since the Tribulation is *especially* the time of God's wrath, and since Christians are not appointed to wrath, then it follows that the church will be raptured *before* the Tribulation..." (*Are We Living in the End Times?* p. 112.) However, reading the verse in context leads to an entirely different conclusion.

The surrounding verses describe the wrath on unbelievers: "destruction will come on them suddenly." The Lord will come like a thief in the night and will take everyone by surprise, destroying the wicked while sparing those who belong to Him. Read the verse here in context:

"Now, brothers, about times and dates we do not need to write to you, for you know very well that the day of the Lord will come like a thief in the night. While people are saying, 'Peace and safety,' destruction will come on them suddenly, as labor pains on a pregnant woman, and they will not escape. But you, brothers, are not in darkness so that this day should surprise you like a thief. You are all sons of the light and sons of the day. We do not belong to the night or to the darkness. So then, let us not be like others, who are asleep, but let us be alert and self-controlled. For those who sleep, sleep at night, and those who get drunk, get drunk at night. But since we belong to the day, let us be self-controlled, putting on faith and love as a breastplate, and the hope of salvation as a helmet. For God did not appoint us to suffer wrath but to receive salvation through our Lord Jesus Christ. He died for us so that, whether we are awake or asleep, we may live together with him." —1 Thess. 5:1-10 NIV

Those who belong to Christ are indeed spared from wrath and go to "live together with him," while those who are left behind have "destruction" come upon them "suddenly," as if surprised by a thief at night. This passage does not show them left alive for a seven-year adventure with a second chance to obtain salvation, as the Left Behind series would have us believe.

Compare 1 Thess. 1:10 and this book's discussion of that verse.

2 Thessalonians 2:1-3

"Concerning the coming of our Lord Jesus Christ and our being gathered to him, we ask you, brothers, not to become easily unsettled or alarmed by some prophecy, report or letter supposed to have come from us, saying that the day of the Lord has already come. Don't let anyone deceive you in any way, for that day will not come until the rebellion occurs and the man of lawlessness is revealed, the man doomed to destruction." (NIV)

The concepts introduced here are widely known by their names as found in the King James Version's rendering of verse three: "Let no man deceive you by any means: for that day shall not come, except there come a falling away first, and that man of sin be revealed, the son of perdition." What is the "falling away," and who is "that man of sin"? Also, what is the timing of these events?

Let's examine each of these elements separately.

THE FALLING AWAY:

The falling away had not yet come when Paul penned these words to the church in Thessalonica, but there is nothing in the passage to indicate that this apostasy from true Christianity still lies in the future from our day. Since the Reformation the traditional Protestant interpretation has been that this falling away climaxed with the elevation of the Bishop of Rome to the office of Pontifex Maximus. This was the title of the high priest of pagan Rome before the Empire; then the Caesars took on the title; finally, with the demise of the Empire and the rise of papal power, Pope Gregory I (c. 540-604 A.D.) took the pagan title upon himself. As a result, the pope today is commonly referred to as the Pontiff.

Along with the pagan title came a host of pagan practices: a hierarchy of priests as mediators between men and God, veneration of saints, the use of images reminiscent of ancient idol worship, transformation of Communion into the mass, the claimed miracle of transubstantiation, and so on.

But Protestant churches have long ago lost the right to point at Roman Catholicism as the great apostasy. Since the 1800s there has been a falling away within Protestantism that has rivaled the sins of Rome. How many churches today stand up for the Bible's creation account in the face of the teaching of evolution? How many condemn the sin of homosexual conduct? For that matter, how often are sermons preached denouncing fornication and adultery? Moreover, the "leaven of Herod" that Jesus warned against (Mark 8:15) has permeated the churches, so that political alliances and financial support from questionable sources cloud the thinking of those who should be preaching the pure Gospel message.

There is no need to wait for a character like *Left Behind*'s Nicolae Carpathia to set up the "Enigma Babylon One World Faith." (See the fourth Left Behind volume: *Soul Harvest: The World Takes Sides* page 212.) Such an organizational oneness with non-Christian religions is not required for a worldwide "falling away" to take place. Today the ecumenical belief that "all roads lead to God" has homogenized the thinking of religious leaders of many major denominations. They gladly join with non-Christian groups to promote "unity" and "acceptance."

In their book *Are We Living in the End Times?* Tim LaHaye and Jerry Jenkins acknowledge that "whole denominations" have already gone into apostasy. (page 77) But they ask, "How close are we?" to a fulfillment of Paul's words above. Instead of admitting that the falling away has already taken place, they point to a future fulfillment in someone like their fictional "Pontifex Maximus Peter" who writes "an official Enigma Babylon declaration" denouncing the Old and New Testaments. (page 67) They say, "All it would take for the world's religions to unite under the leadership of Rome would be the Rapture of all true Christians." (page 177)

The facts show, however, that the falling away began centuries ago and has blossomed so fully in our day that it is easy to see why Jesus asked, "when the Son of Man comes, will He really find faith on the earth?" (Luke 18:8 NKJV) There is no need to wait for another falling away, as Left Behind teaches.

THE MAN OF SIN:

Like most scholars, the authors of Left Behind identify the "man of sin" or "man of lawlessness" with the Antichrist. They speak of "the Antichrist in 2 Thessalonians 2:3, where he is called 'the man of sin . . . the son of perdition.'" (*Are We Living in the End Times*, p. 273) This, however, is an inference, not an established fact. The fact is that the word "antichrist" appears only in the first and second epistles of John— nowhere else!—and is used there mainly in the plural. (See the discussion of 1 John 2:18 later in this book.)

Because "Satan entered Judas" (Luke 22:3) and Judas, too, is called "the son of perdition" (John 17:12), LaHaye and Jenkins conclude that there will be a single individual man who will fulfill the role of Antichrist, that "the Antichrist is indwelt by the devil," and that "after the devil is defeated by the angelic forces and forcibly ejected from heaven at the mid-point of the Tribulation, he enters the body of the Antichrist." (*ibid*, p. 273) Many scholars agree with this, too, but it likewise is an inference drawn from circumstantial similarities, not an established fact.

That being said, the fact remains that the "man of sin" was identified as the Pope by John Calvin, Martin Luther and other great preachers of the Reformation, as well as by most Protestant teachers until after the mid-1800s. The Westminster Confession of Faith (1646-1647) declared, "There is no other head of the Church, but the Lord Jesus Christ; nor can the Pope of Rome, in any sense, be head thereof; but is that Antichrist, that man of sin, and son of perdition, that exalteth himself, in the Church..." (chapter 25, section 6) According to Albert Barnes (1798-1870), "Most Protestant commentators have referred it to the great apostasy under the Papacy, and, by the 'man of sin'... an allusion to the Roman Pontiff, the Pope." (*Notes on the New Testament*, 2 Thess. 2:3) As we saw above, Luther taught that "St. Paul prophesied all this, when in 2 Thess. 2, 3-4, he calls him: 'The man of sin and the son of perdition'" and applied the passage to the papacy. (Martin Luther's "Sermon for the Twenty-Fifth Sunday after Trinity; Matthew 24:15-28" from his *Church Postil*, first published in 1525.)

John Owen (English church leader, 1613-1683) wrote "Papal usurpation upon these offices of Christ manifests the pope to be the Man of Sin." (*Two Short Catechisms*, Chap. XI. — Of the Offices of Christ; and, First, of His Kingly) The London Baptist Confession of faith (1677/1689) declared, "The Lord Jesus Christ is the Head of the Church...neither can the Pope of Rome in any sense be head thereof, but is that Antichrist, that Man of sin, and Son of perdition, that exalteth himself in the Church against Christ..."

How do hundreds of years of Protestant tradition stack up against the new thinking of the dispensationalists? Is there reason to attach greater weight to the word of Tim LaHaye and Jerry Jenkins than to the word of Martin Luther, John Calvin, Roger Williams, John Knox, Jonathan Edwards, John Wesley, William Tyndale, John Wycliffe, John Huss, and the 1646 Westminster Confession of Faith? All of these affirmed that the Pope was the prophesied "man of sin."

THE TIMING OF THESE EVENTS:

This passage in Thessalonians poses an insurmountable problem for those who advocate the Left Behind view of the end times, because it shows the "man of sin" appearing *before* the Rapture: "the coming of our Lord Jesus Christ and our being gathered to him ...will not come until the rebellion occurs and the man of lawlessness is revealed."

Since Left Behind theology teaches that Christ returns twice, once invisibly at the Rapture and again seven years later at the Glorious Appearing, we must first identify where these writings place "the coming of our Lord" referred to in the passage above. It is very clear. When apologists for the novels separate verses into two lists, they do not place this passage under the heading "Second Coming" or Glorious Appearing, but instead they list "2 Thessalonians 2:1, 3" under "Rapture." (*The Truth*

Behind Left Behind by Mark Hitchcock and Thomas Ice, with Introduction by Tim LaHaye, p. 36)

This poses a problem, however, for believers in Left Behind, because the passage goes on to say that the coming of the Lord and our being gathered to him won't happen "except there come a falling away first, and that man of sin be revealed." So, Paul has the "man of sin" being revealed *before* the Rapture. Left Behind has the Rapture first, and then the "man of sin" revealed during the following seven years.

Perhaps this clear contradiction of their beliefs may explain why, when LaHaye and Jenkins quote 2 Thessalonians 2:1-3 on page 69 of *Are We Living in the End Times*, they conveniently stop in mid-sentence without finishing. They quote the part of verse 3 that says, "Don't let anyone deceive you in any way, for that day will not come *until the rebellion occurs*" and stop there, with a period for punctuation, omitting the rest of the sentence, "and the man of lawlessness is revealed, the man doomed to destruction." Perhaps they drop that part of the sentence, because it shows that the Rapture does not occur until *after* the man of lawlessness is revealed.

The biblical sequence of events is no problem at all, though, for the traditional view of the "man of sin" held by Luther, Calvin, and the other Reformers. If he is indeed the pope, as they taught, then he appeared well before "the coming of the Lord and our being gathered to him."

(NOTE: On page 99 of *Are We Living in the End Times?* LaHaye and Jenkins list 2 Thessalonians 2:1 under "Rapture Passages", but they fail to include verse 3. Then on page 111 of the same book they apply the entire passage to "the Glorious Appearing"—*not* the Rapture—thus contradicting its designation under the heading "Rapture" a few pages earlier as well as in *The Truth Behind Left Behind*, as noted above This confusion is further evidence against their attempt to divide the Second Coming into two separate events seven years apart. Those who try to make this artificial distinction are bound to trip themselves up doing so, as happened here.)

2 Thessalonians 2:4

"Who opposeth and exalteth himself above all that is called God, or that is worshipped; so that he as God sitteth

in the temple of God, shewing himself that he is God."
(KJV)

The *New International Version* puts it this way: "He will oppose and will exalt himself over everything that is called God or is worshiped, so that he sets himself up in God's temple, proclaiming himself to be God." (NIV)

This verse serves as the basis for the Left Behind teaching that the Jews will rebuild the temple of God in Jerusalem. After all, how could someone sit in the temple or set himself up in God's temple and proclaim himself to be God, unless the temple were rebuilt? "Clearly, if the temple is to be desecrated at that point, it must be built earlier," say LaHaye and Jenkins in *Are We Living in the End Times?* (page 123)

Yes, that could be a logical conclusion *if* Paul was referring to the Jerusalem temple. But Paul wrote elsewhere, "Don't you know that you yourselves are God's temple and that God's Spirit lives in you? If anyone destroys God's temple, God will destroy him; for God's temple is sacred, and you are that temple." (1 Cor. 3:16-17) So, perhaps he was speaking here, too, of the spiritual temple—Christ's church—rather than a reconstructed building in Jerusalem.

Cyril of Jerusalem, who lived from 315 to 386 A.D., quoted from 2 Thessalonians 2 and then wrote, "'So that he seateth himself in the temple of God.' What temple then? He means, the Temple of the Jews which has been destroyed. For God forbid that it should be the one in which we are!" (Lecture 15, paragraph 15) So, it occurred to Christian writers very early on that Paul might have meant that 'the man of sin' would be seated in the spiritual temple, the Church, and that possibility frightened them. "God forbid . . . !" Cyril exclaimed.

That Paul spoke of the spiritual temple, the Church, is the view that was held almost universally for centuries by Protestant preachers. Colonial American Congregationalist theologian and missionary Jonathan Edwards (1703-1758) expressed it this way: "And it is prophesied, that this man of sin should set himself up in the temple or visible church of God, pretending to be vested with divine power, as head of the church, (2 Thess. ii. 4.) And all this is exactly come to pass in the church of Rome." (*A History of the Work of Redemption*)

As noted above in our discussion of 1 Corinthians 3:16-17, Martin Luther understood it this way: that Paul referred to the spiritual temple in connection with the 'man of sin,' rather than a rebuilt Jewish temple in Jerusalem. Luther said in his sermon (quoted more fully above) that "it cannot be understood otherwise than of the new spiritual temple, which as he [Paul] says himself, we are," and that the 'man of sin' is the pope who elevates himself to god-like status in the spiritual temple, the Church. Luther also noted in this sermon that supporters of the papacy argue for fulfillment in a rebuilt Jewish temple, to point the finger away from the pope: "the Papists want to turn this passage from themselves and say: Christ and Paul are speaking of the temple of Jerusalem, that Antichrist shall sit and rule there." (Luther's "Sermon for the Twenty-Fifth Sunday after Trinity; Matthew 24:15-28" from his *Church Postil*)

Left Behind's view of the papacy contrasts strongly with Luther's. In fact, the fifth novel in the series indicates that pope at the time of the Rapture is a true disciple of Christ. The pope is not among those 'left behind' like the assistant pastor of New Hope church. Rather, the papacy is vacant briefly when the pope disappears in the Rapture. (*Apollyon: The Destroyer Is Unleashed*, page 53)

But, even if Paul did mean to refer to 'the man of sin' sitting in the physical temple in Jerusalem, this would not necessarily argue for a future rebuilding project during a coming seven-year tribulation; this would not be necessary if the temple has already been rebuilt. Could it be that the third temple has already been built, but that we have failed to recognize it? That notion may seem absurd. But consider a similar situation: The long-awaited Messiah appeared, and the people who had been waiting for him failed to recognize him. They expected a king, and he came as a carpenter's son; they expected a royal birth, and he was born in a stable; they expected a conquering liberator, but he died on a cross. No wonder they failed to recognize him! Could it be that the temple has already been rebuilt, but students of prophecy have failed to recognize it?

As a matter of fact, a temple does now occupy Temple Mount in Jerusalem. It is called the Dome of the Rock and bears an inscription saying it was built by "the servant of God Abd al-Malik Ibn Marwan, emir of the faithful, in the year seventy-two." (72 in the Muslim calendar is 691-692 A.D.) Do the builders and maintainers of the Dome fit the biblical description of an Antichrist? The inscriptions on the walls of this temple make bold declarations about Jesus Christ. Are they the sort of statements we should expect of an Antichrist? Consider these, which appear prominently displayed in Arabic, and notice that they deny that Jesus is the Son of God:

"Oh God, bless Your Messenger and Your servant Jesus son of Mary. Peace be on him the day he was born, and the day he dies, and the day he shall be raised alive!"

"God is only One God. Far be it removed from His transcendent majesty that He should have a son."

"The Messiah, Jesus son of Mary, was only a Messenger of God, and His Word which He conveyed unto Mary, and a spirit from Him."

"Such was Jesus, son of Mary... It befitteth not God that He should take unto Himself a son."

"Praise be to God, Who hath not taken unto Himself a son."

Notice how closely these inscriptions fit he Apostle John's definition of an Antichrist as "the man who denies that Jesus is the Christ. Such a man is the antichrist—he denies the Father and the Son. No one who denies the Son has the Father." (1 John 2:22-23) So, could this Dome of the Rock, which sits in the place of God's temple on Temple Mount in Jerusalem, be Antichrist's temple? Before dismissing the possibility, consider that the Islamic occupier of Temple Mount was identified as Antichrist in the writings of both John Calvin and Martin Luther.

Calvin saw the Pope and "Mahomet" as "the two horns of the Antichrist." One sat in the spiritual temple, the Church, and the other occupied the place God had chosen for himself on Temple Mount. Calvin wrote, "Lyke as Mahomet saith ty his Alcoran is ye soveraine wisdome, so saith the Pope of his owne decrees: For they be the two hornes of Antichrist." (*The Sermons of M. John Calvin upon the Fifth Booke of Moses called Deuteronomie*, translated by Arthur Golding, first published in London, 1583, from a facsimile reprint by Banner of Truth Trust, 1987.)

Calvin also wrote, "Paul, however, does not speak of one individual, but of a kingdom, that was to be taken possession of by Satan, that he might set up a seat of abomination in the midst of God's temple — which we see accomplished in Popery. The revolt, it is true, has spread more widely, for Mahomet, as he was an apostate, turned away the Turks, his followers, from Christ." (*Commentary on Philippians, Colossians, and Thessalonians*)

If Calvin saw the papacy and Islam as two "horns" of the antichrist, Martin Luther saw them as "legs" of the same antichrist. (*Luther's Works*, Weimer ed., 53, 394f.) Luther added, "the Pope is the spirit of antichrist, and the Turk is the flesh of antichrist. They help each other in their murderous work. The latter slaughters bodily by the sword; and the former spiritually by doctrine." (Luther's *Tischreden*, Weimer ed., 1, No. 330)

So, whether one understands 'the man of sin' to sit in the spiritual temple, the Church, or in a physical temple on Temple Mount in Jerusalem—or both—there is no reason to wait for a future antichrist character like Left Behind's Nicolae Carpathia to build another temple.

See, also, the discussion of Matthew 24:15-16 and 1 Corinthians 3:16-17.

2 Thessalonians 2:6-8

> "And now you know what is holding him back, so that he may be revealed at the proper time. For the secret power of lawlessness is already at work; but the one who now holds it back will continue to do so till he is taken out of the way. And then the lawless one will be revealed, whom the Lord Jesus will overthrow with the breath of his mouth and destroy by the splendor of his coming." (NIV)

If the "man of sin" were Left Behind's antichrist figure, Nicolae Carpathia, with the Church holding him back, it is hard to imagine his power being "already at work" when Paul wrote to the Thessalonian congregation. But if the traditional Protestant understanding is meant, then Paul's comments make more sense.

"Bishop Newton maintains that the foundations of popery were laid in the apostle's days, and that the superstructure was raised by degrees; and this is entirely in accordance with the statements of the apostle Paul," according to the commentary on these verses in *Barnes Notes* (1884-85 edition) by Albert Barnes. "This was kept in check as long as Rome was the seat of the imperial power," Barnes continues. After the Roman empire's secular power was taken out of the way, the pope was able to hold sway—and Islam was able to rise in the east.

Commenting on this passage in his *Commentary on Philippians, Colossians, and Thessalonians*, Calvin, too, explains how the iniquity was already at work:

> "The mystery of iniquity. This is opposed to revelation; for as Satan had not yet gathered so much strength, as that Antichrist could openly oppress the Church, he says that he is carrying on secretly and clandestinely what he would do openly in his own time. He was therefore at that time secretly laying the foundations on which he would afterwards rear the edifice, as actually took place. And this tends to confirm more fully what I have already stated, that it is not one individual that is represented under the term Antichrist, but one kingdom, which extends itself through many ages. In the same sense, John says that Antichrist will come, but that there were already many in his time. (1 John 2:18.) For he admonishes those who were then living to be on their guard against that deadly pestilence, which was at that time shooting up in various forms. For sects were rising up which were the seeds, as it were, of that unhappy weed which has well-nigh choked and destroyed God's entire tillage."

So, Calvin saw evidence of the antichrist's kingdom at work long before the papacy took power. Rather than the Roman empire holding it back, however, Calvin's view, as explained in the same *Commentary*, was that "the light of the gospel must be diffused though all parts of the earth before God would thus give loose reins to Satan," and so it was the need for the Word to be spread first that was the restraining factor. Yet the timing proved to be the same.

The majority view, however was that the Roman Empire was the force holding back the Antichrist. This understanding was already common in the early Church, even while Rome still ruled. "What obstacle is there but the Roman state, the falling away of which, by being scattered into ten kingdoms, shall introduce Antichrist upon (its own ruins)?" wrote Tertullian (145 to 220 A.D.) in *De Resurrectione Carnis (On The Resurrection of the Flesh)*. Cyril of Jerusalem (315 to 386 A.D.) wrote, "But this aforesaid Antichrist is to come when the times of the Roman empire shall have been fulfilled... There shall rise up together ten kings of the Romans... and after these an eleventh, the Antichrist, who by his magical craft shall seize upon the Roman power." (*Catechetical Lectures,* Lecture XV)

So, for nearly two thousand years—from Tertullian to Albert Barnes— the common view was that the Roman Empire was the force holding back the Antichrist from appearing, an antichrist whose power was already at work in Paul's day and whose full manifestation was found later in the rise of papal power.

2 Thessalonians 2:9-10

> The coming of the lawless one will be in accordance with the work of Satan displayed in all kinds of counterfeit miracles, signs and wonders, and in every sort of evil that deceives those who are perishing. They perish because they refused to love the truth and so be saved. (NIV)

This has its fulfillment during a coming seven-year tribulation, according to Left Behind teaching. "Satan will go all out with deceiving spirits and signs and lying wonders potent enough almost to deceive even 'the very elect.' ...that period has not yet come," according to LaHaye and Jenkins. (*Are We Living in the End Times?* page 35) In their novels the antichrist Nicolae Carpathia has his right-hand man "Most High Reverend Father [Leon] Fortunato" send out miracle workers to deceive the world. (*The Remnant,* page 318)

But there is no reason to look to the future for such deception. There has been plenty of it already down through history—enough counterfeit miracles to get all of Christendom to follow the Bishop of Rome for many centuries. "It is hardly necessary to remark that the papacy has always relied for support on its pretended miracles," says *Barnes Notes* when commenting on these verses. After mentioning specific miracles claimed for various relics and shrines, Barnes adds, "In addition to these and all similar pretensions, there is the power claimed of performing a miracle at the pleasure of the priest by the change of bread and wine into 'the body and blood, the soul and divinity' of the Lord Jesus. ...The power of working miracles has been one of the standing claims of the Papacy."

So there is no need to look to a future seven-year tribulation for fulfillment of these prophetic verses.

Titus 2:13

> **while we wait for the blessed hope—the glorious appearing of our great God and Savior, Jesus Christ (NIV)**

In his book Rapture Under Attack Tim LaHaye declares that "Christians are not waiting for the Glorious Appearing." (page 51) Yet, Paul wrote to Titus above that "we" are waiting for the glorious appearing. Since Paul and Titus were Christians and were looking forward to this event, LaHaye's statement contradicts Scripture.

In the same book LaHaye comments on Titus 2:13 to the effect that "Paul's 'blessed hope' is the Rapture, for it is unique to the church. No one else will take part in it. ...The Glorious Appearing, on the other hand, is not for the Christian but for the remnant at the end of the Tribulation." (pages 68-69) Thus, LaHaye inserts a gap of seven years between the "blessed hope" and the "glorious appearing" of Christ.

Does Titus 2:13 really refer to two separate events, seven years apart, as LaHaye claims? Clearly not, according to the New International Version's rendering of the verse quoted above, which equates the two expressions: "the blessed hope-the glorious appearing." Translators of the New Living Translation likewise show it to be a single event: "while we look forward to that wonderful event when the glory of our great God and Savior, Jesus Christ, will be revealed."

Bible commentator Robert Jamieson wrote that in this verse, "There is but one Greek article to both 'hope' and 'appearing,' which marks their close connection (the hope being about to be realized only at the appearing of Christ)." (Commentary Critical and Explanatory on the Whole Bible, 1871) That is why translators commonly present the blessed hope and glorious appearing of Christ as a single event,. Even the founder of dispensationalism, John Nelson Darby, appears to have followed this grammatical rule in the translation he himself produced, rendering Titus 2:13, "awaiting the blessed hope and appearing of the glory of our great God and Saviour Jesus Christ."

Matthew Henry commented on Titus 2:13 to the effect that the blessed hope would be attained "At, and in, the glorious appearing of Christ" when he explained it this way in his *Commentary on the Whole Bible*: "By hope is meant the thing hoped for, namely, Christ himself, who is called our hope (1 Tim. i. 1), and blessedness in and through him, even riches of glory (Eph. i. 18), hence fitly termed here that blessed hope. ... At, and in, the glorious appearing of Christ will the blessed hope of Christians be attained; for their felicity will be this, To be where he is, and to behold his glory, John xvii. 24."

2 Peter 3:12

"waiting for and hastening the coming of the day of God" (RSV)

The black Honda Civic that I drive every day sports a bumper sticker that tastefully proclaims, "Jesus is coming soon." Jesus admonished, "Therefore keep watch, because you do not know on what day your Lord will come." (Matt. 24:42 NIV) Peter urged similar eager watchfulness above. I would have expected the Left Behind series to do the same. But, instead of portraying the return of Christ as imminent, LaHaye and Jenkins put it off perhaps fifty or more years from now. It is nothing that people living today need to worry about; perhaps our children will see it, according to their chronology.

This pushing off of the Lord's coming into the latter half of the twenty-first century is not clearly discernable in the original *Left Behind* novel, nor in the eleven volumes that followed it. They offer no substantial clues to the setting, except that it is in modern times. The nonfiction volume by the same authors titled *Are We Living in the End Times?* suggests we will see "the United Nations the ruling force of the world by at least 2025—and maybe much sooner!" (p. 170) But the Left Behind prequel titled *The Rising: Antichrist is Born*, released in March 2005, moves the time of Christ's return out by several decades:

Nicolae Carpathia, the coming Antichrist, had not yet been born, but his parents Sorin and Marilena in Romania "were the only couple she knew who still owned a television receiver that did not hang on the wall." Their "flat-screen" TV was ridiculed as a shamefully "old set." (*The Rising*, p. 20) And that was before Carpathia was born, so his rule as Antichrist would have to be decades farther into the future.

When Rayford Steele was just nine years old, and his friends' families all had the latest model automobiles, he lamented over his parents' old Chevy: "Cars simply weren't supposed to look like they aged anymore. But everybody knew, because the auto manufacturers now had only two ways to make cars look new: they changed styles every year, and color schemes changed every three or four years. ...There was the silver and platinum phase when cars were designed to look like classics from the first decade of the new century. Then came the primary colors, which didn't last long—except for that Chevy." (*The Rising*, p. 14) So, the setting is at least far enough into the future that cars from the first decade of our twenty-first century are considered classics. Add to that the thirty-five or forty years that pass as Rayford Steel matures into the character of the later novels in the series, and it becomes plain that LaHaye and Jenkins portray the return of Christ as not happening until the latter half of this century—decades, perhaps a lifetime into the future, for those who now read their books.

Thus the Left Behind novels fail to convey the urgency that Peter stressed above. Despite the books' admonitions to accept Christ before the Rapture, the authors place that event so far in the future that readers are given the impression that they have decades to decide—plus an additional seven years after the Rapture, if they choose to hedge their bets.

1 John 2:18

"Dear children, this is the last hour; and as you have heard that the antichrist is coming, even now many antichrists have come. This is how we know it is the last hour." (NIV)

In the Left Behind novels the character Nicolae Carpathia is "the Antichrist." But does Scripture teach us to look for such an individual?

Many Bible translations refer to *the* antichrist or *the* Antichrist in this verse: *New King James Version, New Living Translation, New International Version*, Young's *Literal Translation, Hebrew Names Version*, and so on. But other translations say simply that "antichrist" is coming, without the definite article: *King James Version, English Standard Version, New American Standard Bible, Revised Standard Version, American Standard Version, J. N. Darby Translation, Noah Webster Version*, and more. *The Jerusalem Bible* actually uses the indefinite article and says, "you were told that an Antichrist must come, and now several antichrists have already appeared."

Like many other commentators, the authors of *Left Behind* conclude that one man will personally fulfill this prophecy, and that he will also be "the man of sin" (2 Thess. 2:3) and the "beast" (Rev. 13:2). But that requires a large leap from what is actually found written in the Word of God. If you read 1 John 2:18-26, 4:1-3 and 2 John 7-11, you will have read everything the Bible says about antichrist(s). And those passages teach that the antichrist is both plural (not a single individual) and already present in John's day; note the portions I have italicized here:

> "you have heard that the antichrist is coming, *even now many antichrists have come. ... They* went out from us, but *they* did not really belong to us. For if *they* had belonged to us, *they* would have remained with us; but *their* going showed that none of *them* belonged to us. ...Who is the liar? It is the man who denies that Jesus is the Christ. *Such a man is the antichrist*—he denies the Father and the Son. ... I am writing these things to you about *those* who *are trying* to lead you astray."— 1 John 2:18-26 NIV

> "Dear friends, do not believe every spirit, but test the spirits to see whether they are from God, because *many* false prophets have gone out into the world. This is how you can recognize the Spirit of God: Every spirit that acknowledges that Jesus Christ has come in the flesh is from God, but every spirit that does not acknowledge Jesus is not from God. *This is the spirit of the antichrist*, which you have heard is coming and *even now is already in the world*."— 1 John 4:1-3 NIV

> "*Many* deceivers, who do not acknowledge Jesus Christ as

coming in the flesh, *have gone out* into the world. *Any such person is the deceiver and the antichrist."*— 2 John 7 NIV

Notice that John referred to "many" antichrists and used the plural pronouns "they" and "them."

A reader encountering these passages in context, without exposure to Left Behind novels or other theological expositions, would hardly conclude that he had to be on the lookout for a future world ruler like Nicolae Carpathia. Rather, he would know anyone denying Christ's coming in the flesh is an antichrist, and that many antichrists existed in John's day. He would also infer that we should beware of such people today, too. Since Scripture says nothing about a particular Antichrist who would rule the world for seven years, one must depend on the interpretations found in other books by other authors to draw such conclusions.

But if there is to be an outstanding Antichrist, as many believe, then why not accept the identification offered by John Calvin and Martin Luther? As we noted above in the discussions of 'the man of sin' (2 Thess. 2:1-3 and 2 Thess. 2:4), Calvin saw the papacy and Islam as the two "horns" of Antichrist and Luther saw them as the two "legs" of Antichrist. Let's look at each 'horn' or 'leg' separately:

THE POPE

Martin Luther declared that "the Pope" is "the true Antichrist, of whom it is written that he sitteth in the temple of God, among the people." (Martin Luther's "Sermon for the Twenty-Fifth Sunday after Trinity; Matthew 24:15-28" from his Church Postil, first published in 1525) John Knox (1514?-1572), the father of the Church of Scotland and Presbyterianism, wrote of "the vanity of the Papistical Religion, and the deceit, pride, and tyranny of that Roman Antichrist." (*History of the Reformation of Religion within the Realm of Scotland* by John Knox, book 4, chapter 1)

But this notion did not arise first in the Reformation of the 1500's. During the early 1200's Eberhard II, archbishop of Salzburg, examined the history of the papacy and drew the same conclusion. In the mid-1300's Michael of Cesena (or Michael Sesenas) declared the Pope to be "Antichrist." John Wycliffe (1320-1384) wrote that "It is supposed, and with much probability, that the Roman pontiff is the great Antichrist." John Huss (1372-1417) declared a century before the Reformation that the pope was "antichrist, or at least the chief and principal minister or vicar of antichrist." And John Calvin joined his contemporary, Luther, in making the same identification.

So, also, did English Bible translator William Tyndale (1490-1536). He is quoted in *Foxe's Book of Martyrs* as asking an acquaintance, "Do you not know that the pope is very Antichrist, whom the Scripture speaketh of? But beware what you say; for if you shall be perceived to be of that opinion, it will cost you your life." And, not long after that, Tyndale did indeed pay with his life. Yet each volume in the Left Behind series bears the name "Tyndale" on the cover, for they are printed and distributed by the modern publisher Tyndale House. If the fiery William Tyndale were alive today, he would no doubt be denouncing this publishing house for attaching his name to a teaching so contrary to what he believed and taught.

As noted above, Roger Williams and John Wesley likewise agreed in attaching the title Antichrist to the papacy, and the 1646 Westminster Confession of Faith confirmed the same teaching. In the late 1800s preacher Charles Spurgeon summed up the prevailing view this way: "Who is this Pope of Rome? His Holiness? Call him not so, but call him His Blasphemy! His Profanity! His Impudence! What are he and his cardinals, and his legates, but the image and incarnation of Antichrist, to be in due time cast with the beast and the false prophet into the lake of fire?" (Spurgeon's *The Treasury of David—Psalm 108*)

So for hundreds and hundreds of years, from Eberhard in the 1200s to Spurgeon in the late 1800s, respected teachers and serious students of the Bible have concluded that the pope is an Antichrist. It was the majority opinion in Protestantism until the early 1900s, and many denominations still hold to this doctrine. Can it be dismissed as some sort of 'anti-Catholic prejudice'?

Why has the pope been identified as Antichrist? Entire books have been written on the topic. I can hardly do it justice here. For more information than is found in this book, please turn to the writings of Luther, Calvin and the Reformers. Their works can be obtained through the inter-library loan desk of most public libraries and can be found online in the Christian Classics Ethereal Library at www.CCEL.org. Their reasoning revolves around the way the papacy has usurped the position of Christ himself. As the London Baptist Confession of 1689 puts it, "The Lord Jesus Christ is the Head of the church, in whom, by the appointment of the Father, all power for the calling, institution, order or government of the church, is invested in a supreme and sovereign manner; neither can the Pope of Rome in any sense be head thereof, but is that antichrist, that man of sin, and son of perdition, that exalteth himself in the church against Christ." The pope's self-exalting titles include Holy Father, Vicar of Christ, Successor of the Prince of the Apostles and Supreme Pontiff of the Universal Church (from Pontifex Maximus, originally the title of pagan high priest of Rome).

Also central to the thinking of those who have identified the papacy with the Antichrist, is the way the popes have enforced their power against ordinary people who studied the Bible and sought to follow Christ instead as head. Over a span of hundreds of years the Inquisition imprisoned, tortured, tried and executed countless thousands of believers. The persecution of Christians by Tim LaHaye's fictional Antichrist, Nicolae Capathia, is bland and mild compared with the real-life horrors of the Inquisition. In the days of Luther and Calvin the smell of roasting human flesh still hung in the air from the flames where men and women were slowly burned alive. Later, stripped of its secular power by Napoleon's conquest at the very end of the 1700s, the papacy began behaving better toward Bible-believers in Catholic lands—much like the Nicolae Carpathia character who, at one point in his career, pretends to be a pacifist and a benefactor. Today's evangelicals seem to have forgotten the papacy's abuses that Spurgeon was certain we would never forget:

> "Whether it may be traced to want of will or want of inclination on the part of other establishments, it is certain that the Popish Antichrist alone has been able to drink of the overflowing blood-cup filled by familiars and tormentors. Long pampered by the state, she came to be its lord and tyrant, using fire and sword, prison and rack, to work her accursed will. The Inquisition was the masterpiece of infernal craft and malice, and its deeds were far more worthy of fiends than men. If the church of Rome could at this moment change its Ethiopian skin for ever, lay aside its leopard's spots, and become a pure community, ten thousand years of immaculate holiness and self-denying philanthropy could not avail to blot out the remembrance of the enormous crimes with which the Inquisition has loaded it. There is a deep and indelible sentence of damnation written upon the apostate church by avenging justice for its more than infernal cruelties, and the curse is registered in heaven; nor can any pretences to present liberality reverse the condemnation which outraged humanity has pronounced against it; its infamy is engraved in the rock for ever. Centuries of the most liberal policy would not convince mankind

that Popery had become tolerant at heart; she wallowed so greedily in oppression, torture, and murder in her palmy days, that the foam of human gore hangs around her wolfish hugs, and men will not believe her to be a gentle lamb, let her bleat as she may. Against her common humanity is up in arms as much as evangelical religion." ("The Inquisition" by C. H. Spurgeon, from the August 1868 *Sword and Trowel* magazine)

Spurgeon was wrong—not about the papacy, but about mankind's memory and even the memory of evangelicals. Just as in our day one church after another is abandoning the biblical view of homosexual practice in favor of 'politically correct' thinking, so during the 1900s the Protestant churches put aside their founders' view of the pope in the name of broad-minded tolerance.   The Left Behind novels have completed this transformation by showing the pope raptured at Christ's return. (*Apollyon: The Destroyer Is Unleashed*, page 53) Character Bruce Barnes, hypocritical assistant pastor of an evangelical church, finds himself left behind, but the Roman pontiff is taken to heaven.

ISLAM

Much less has been written about the role of Islam, perhaps because Christian writers down through the centuries had far less direct interaction with the followers of Mohammed than they did with the pope and his hierarchy. Still, as noted above, Luther and Calvin wrote of Islam as one of the "legs" or "horns" of Antichrist, the pope being the other leg or horn.

But, if the pope has made himself an Antichrist by elevating himself to Christ's place, by taking upon himself vain titles and by bringing pagan practices and doctrines into the church, Antichrist's other 'leg' has been much more direct in openly denying Christ. Islam is, in fact, the only major world religion based on a foundation of refuting Christian belief. While Buddhism and Hinduism affirm their own doctrines and teachings, Islam started out from the very beginning agreeing with Christians that Jesus was a representative sent by God, while denying that he was God's Son.

Jesus is discussed over and over again throughout the Muslim holy book, the *Koran*, where he is called "Isa, the son of Marium" (Jesus, the son of Mary). The Koran admonishes Mohammed's followers to believe in the revelation given by God "to Abraham, Ishmael, Isaac, Jacob, and the Tribes, and that given to Moses and Jesus." (2:136) It says that Jesus was sent by God, empowered to do miracles and strengthened through

106

the Holy Spirit. (2:87, 253) It acknowledges that he healed lepers, gave sight to the blind and raised the dead by the power of God. (5:110) It affirms that Jesus was born of a virgin, and that he was crucified, rose from the dead, and was taken up to God's presence. (19:20; 4:157-158) But then Islam goes on to deny that Jesus is the only-begotten Son of God, and instead lowers him to a position on a par with all the other prophets. So, it is actually an apostasy from Christianity, and therefore fits John's description of "antichrists" who "went out from among us." Moreover, Islam forbids its subjects from becoming followers of Jesus, from accepting him as their Lord and Savior. Those who do embrace Christ face intense persecution, prison and even death.

If the papacy has earned the title of Antichrist, then Islam deserves this title even more so, especially in our day. Using the Inquisition and other instruments, the papacy put thousands of Bible-believers to death for their faith over the centuries, and today Islam does the same to any who dare preach the Gospel or embrace Christ within its borders. As noted earlier, Calvin compared Islam and the papacy this way: "The revolt, it is true, has spread more widely, for Mahomet, as he was an apostate, turned away the Turks, his followers, from Christ." Calvin elaborated that "the sect of Mahomet was like a violent bursting forth of water, that took away about the half of the Church by its violence. It remained, also, that Antichrist should infect the remaining part with his poison." (Calvin's *Commentaries on the Epistles of Paul to the Philippians, Colossians, and Thessalonians*) See also the article "Calvin on Islam" by Rev. Dr. Francis Nigel Lee at http://www.dr-fnlee.org/docs6/calvislam/calvislam.pdf)

Jude 1:14-15

"And Enoch also, the seventh from Adam, prophesied of these, saying, Behold, the Lord cometh with ten thousands of his saints, To execute judgment upon all..." (KJV)

Supporters of the Left Behind theory use this verse to 'prove' that Christ returns twice, seven years apart. They argue that he returns *for* his saints at the Rapture, and returns *with* his saints seven years later to execute judgment on the wicked. Thus in *The Truth Behind Left Behind* apologists Hitchcock and Ice cite Jude 1:14 with the caption, "Christ comes with His saints." (page 37)

Can they seriously claim that "Enoch...the seventh from Adam" had in mind raptured Christians returning with Christ? God evidently gave a preview of the coming judgment to Enoch, who lived before the flood of Noah's day, long before ancient Israel, and very long before Christ called out his Church. So, does Scripture indicate that Enoch was also given details about Christian believers being raptured so that they could return with Christ seven years later?

The word rendered "saints" here in the King James Version is the Greek *HAGIOS* which is also rendered "holy" in the expression "Holy Spirit" and in references to holy places, things, people and angels. Since Enoch lived before either the Jewish or the Christian congregation came into existence, he would likely have had holy angels in mind, rather than Jewish or Christian saints. Many commentaries make that observation. And this would be fully in harmony with Matthew 25:31: "When the Son of man shall come in his glory, and all the holy angels with him..." (KJV)

Matthew Henry's *Commentary* says that the holy ones include "both angels and the spirits of just men made perfect." According to Barnes' *Notes*, "The word *saints* we now apply commonly to *redeemed* saints, or to Christians. The original word is, however, applicable to all who are *holy*, angels as well as men. The common representation in the Scriptures is, that he would come attended by the angels (Matt. xxv. 31,) and there is doubtless allusion here to such beings."

But, even if Enoch was indeed privileged to foresee the raptured Church here, this still would not necessitate a seven-year gap between the Rapture and Christ's coming to execute judgment. Christians who "meet the Lord in the air" (1 Thess. 4: 17) at his coming are not meeting him to turn him around and send him in the other direction. He keeps coming, with risen saints now accompanying him, too, along with the angels.

Revelation 1:1

"The Revelation of Jesus Christ, which God gave Him to show His servants—things which must shortly take place. And He sent and signified it by His angel to His servant John" (NKJV)

Like the authors of *Left Behind,* I am compelled to understand the Bible literally. (Compare *Are We Living in the End Times?* page 4) It has proven itself to be the inerrant Word of God, so it would be a grievous sin to dismiss what God says by interpreting it to be allegorical or symbolic of something else. By the same token, it would be inappropriate to attach a literal meaning to something that the divine Author of the Bible intended to be taken symbolically.

Sometimes the Bible uses figures of speech or symbolism without plainly declaring the language to be such. For example, in Isaiah 55:12, "all the trees of the field shall clap their hands." (KJV) The prophet did not find it necessary to explain that trees don't have hands and therefore cannot literally clap; the reader understands that the language is poetic or symbolic without an explicit statement to that effect. Similarly, when Jesus said, "the stars shall fall from heaven" (Matt. 24:29) he was speaking as the very One who had created the universe (John 1:10) and clearly knew that heavenly bodies much larger than the earth cannot literally fall.

The presence of figurative language notwithstanding, there are still rules that govern interpretation. The reader or commentator is not free to attach whatever meaning suits his fancy. Symbols must be understood consistently.   When, in Daniel chapter 7, the first beast is a government (Babylon), the second beast is a government (Medo-Persia), the third beast is a government (Greece), the next beast cannot be the Devil or a man named Nicolae Carpathia.

The Revelation or Apocalypse of John was "signified" (Rev. 1:1 KJV) or presented using "signs and symbols" (*Barnes' Notes*). John was told to "write on a scroll *what you see.*" (1:11 NIV) And then he saw a long series of signs and symbols: "A great and wondrous sign appeared in heaven" (12:1 NIV), "Then another sign appeared in heaven" (12:3 NIV), "And I saw another sign in heaven" (15:1 KJV) The meanings of these signs and symbols have been the subject of debate for centuries. I don't expect to be able to settle those debates here.

However, the authors of Left Behind violate the principles of sound biblical interpretation when they arbitrarily switch back and forth between symbolism and literalism. At a whim, they present some of the things John "saw" as literal, physical realities, but others as mere symbols.

For example, they show characters in their novels fighting-off actual locusts that look like battle-armored horses with men's faces and crowns on their heads. (See the discussion of Rev. 9:1-9, below.) Yet, the seven-headed beast from the sea is taken symbolically. (See the discussion of Rev. 13:1-3) Why not also show characters waging war against a literal seven-headed beast? They present the four horsemen of Revelation 6:1-4 as "symbolic." (*Nicolae*, p. 347), but when character Rayford Steele encounters the two hundred million horsemen of Revelation 9:16-19, these are presented as real "horses, not ten feet from him—huge, monstrous, muscular things twice the size of any he had ever seen." (*Assassins*, p. 127)

Such switching back and forth from literal to symbolic to literal again is not a sound approach to interpreting the signs and symbols of the Apocalypse.

Revelation 3:10

"Because thou hast kept the word of my patience, I also will keep thee from the hour of temptation, which shall come upon all the world, to try them that dwell upon the earth." (KJV)

"One of the best promises guaranteeing the church's rapture before the Tribulation is found in Revelation 3:10," say authors LaHaye and Jenkins in *Are We Living in the End Times?* (p. 107) Arguing that the church in Philadelphia to whom these words are addressed pictures "the present-day Bible-believing church," they go on to say, "This verse teaches that the faithful church of the open door, which will not deny His name but will practice good works, evangelism, and missions, will be kept 'out of' the hour of trial (the Great Tribulation) that shall try the whole earth." (pp. 108-109)

Scripture does not say, however, that the Great Tribulation (Greek *megas thlipsis*) is the same as the "temptation" (Greek *peirasmos*) that the church in Philadelphia would be kept from. The word used here is the same as in "lead us not into *temptation*" (Luke 11:4) and "there hath no *temptation* taken you but such as is common to man: but God is faithful, who will not suffer you to be tempted above that ye are able; but will with the *temptation* also make a way to escape, that ye may be able to bear it." (1 Cor. 10:13) God is always faithful to keep those who are truly His from temptation. It is a huge leap to claim this verse refers to a future seven-year tribulation.

Albert Barnes comments in his *Notes*, "This does not mean that they would be kept from calamity of all kinds, but that they would be kept from the *temptation of apostasy* in calamity. He would give them grace to bear up under trials with a Christian spirit, in such a manner that their salvation should not be endangered. . . . The persecutions in the Roman empire would furnish abundant occasions for such a trial."

A Christian woman wrote to Left Behind's authors, objecting that Jesus spoke those words to the ancient church in Philadelphia, rather than concerning a future Great Tribulation, but they state in *Are We Living in the End Times?* that they "wrote her back and suggested it *couldn't* mean that little church, because it was completely destroyed by the Turkish invasion in 1382, long before 'the hour of trial which shall come upon the whole world'"! That period still has not come!" (p. 108) So, they used the supposed future Tribulation to 'prove' that this verse speaks of a future Tribulation—truly an example of circular reasoning.

Revelation 6:1

"...the Lamb opened one of the seals, and I heard..." (KJV)

The Left Behind novels present the seven seal judgments—conquest, war, famine, death, earthquakes, and so on—as literal catastrophes during the first half of a seven year tribulation period. However, as has been shown throughout this book, the tribulation is not a future event, but has already been fulfilled upon the Jewish people and/or the Church. What about the seal judgments then? From the vantage point of eternity, we may look back to realize that we lived through the seal judgments in the years running up to Christ's return. They may have been fulfilled by wars, epidemics and natural disasters of the twentieth and twenty-first centuries. Or, we may find these judgments compressed into the climactic wrath of the Lamb at Armageddon. But there is no biblical basis for asserting, as the Left Behind series does, that the seven seals mean unbelievers will go through a long ordeal affording them a "second chance" after Christ returns to rapture the Church.

> When the Lamb opened the second seal, I heard the second living creature say, "Come!" Then another horse came out, a fiery red one. Its rider was given power to take peace away from the earth and to make men slay each other. To him was given a large sword. (NIV)

The third novel in the Left Behind series, *Nicolae: The Rise of Antichrist*, declares "this is a prediction of global war. It will likely become known as World War III. It will be instigated by the Antichrist, and yet he will rise as the great resolver of it, the great peacemaker, as he is the great deceiving liar." (p. 320)

Does the rider of the red horse point to World War III, or has his ride been fulfilled by the two world wars that dominated the twentieth century? The First World War took peace away from the earth and led directly to the Balfour Declaration which laid the groundwork for the return of Jews to the Holy Land. The Second World War took peace away from the earth and saw a nearly-successful attempt to exterminate the Jewish people, followed by the actual re-establishment of the state of Israel.

The confident assertion of the Left Behind authors notwithstanding, there is not enough evidence in Scripture to be certain which world war is meant here—a future conflict, or the world wars we have already seen.

Revelation 7:3

> "Hurt not the earth, neither the sea, nor the trees, till we have sealed the servants of our God in their foreheads." (KJV)

In the middle of the fourth volume of the Left Behind series, *Soul Harvest: The World Takes Sides*, characters Mac and Rayford notice smudges on each other's foreheads "like what Catholics used to get on Ash Wednesday." (page 171) Looking more closely, they notice that each actually has a raised or embossed cross on his forehead—"visible only to other believers." Character Tsion Ben Judah goes on to identify it: "The seventh chapter of Revelation tells of 'the servants of our God being sealed on their foreheads. That has to be what this is!'" (pages 193-194) From this point on during the novels' tribulation period, believers are able to identify others who share their faith by this mark.

A similar sealing in the forehead was described in the Old Testament. Hypocrisy and outright idolatry were prevalent in the corrupt Jewish congregation, and God showed his prophet Ezekiel a vision in which faithful individuals received a mark on their foreheads: "And he called to the man clothed with linen, which had the writer's inkhorn by his side; And the LORD said unto him, Go through the midst of the city, through the midst of Jerusalem, and set a mark upon the foreheads of the men that sigh and that cry for all the abominations that be done in the midst thereof." (Ezek.9:3-4 KJV) Everyone without the mark was to be killed by angelic executioners. However, history does not record any visible marking or sealing in the forehead in Ezekiel's day. The mark Ezekiel spoke of was visible only to God and his holy angels.

Does the Bible really indicate that modern servants of God who are "sealed" during the final days of this world will display a visible cross or other mark, as the Left Behind series teaches? Paul writes that believers are "sealed with the Holy Spirit of promise" and advises us, "do not grieve the Holy Spirit of God, by whom you were sealed." (Eph. 1:13, 4:30 NKJV) Would we expect God to abandon such sealing with the Holy Spirit, and use instead some visible identifying mark?

There is no biblical basis to expect such a visible mark to appear on the faces of believers. Jesus said, "By this shall all men know that ye are my disciples, if ye have love one to another." (John 13:35 KJV) Love is one of the fruits of the Spirit. (Gal. 5:22) Christ said that his true followers could identify impostors "by their fruits." (Matt. 7:16, 20)

Would these standards for identifying believers be replaced in the end times by a visible mark that would be indisputable? That certainly seems unlikely in view of Jesus' reference to many impostors who would masquerade successfully as Christians right up until the last day: "Many will say to me in that day, Lord, Lord, have we not prophesied in thy name? and in thy name have cast out devils? and in thy name done many wonderful works? And then will I profess unto them, I never knew you: depart from me, ye that work iniquity." (Matt. 7:22-23 KJV) Such a masquerade right up until the Judgment would be impossible if a visible seal marked those who belonged to Christ as Left Behind teaches.

> "And the seven angels who had the seven trumpets prepared themselves to sound. The first angel sounded, and there followed hail and fire mingled with blood, and they were cast upon the earth; and the third part of trees was burnt up, and all green grass was burnt up." (KJV)

A third of the trees and grass are burned up; a third of the sea is turned to blood and a third of the creatures and ships destroyed; a third of the waters are poisoned by wormwood; a third of the sun, moon and stars are darkened; locusts with scorpion-like tails torment unbelievers. As with the seven seals of Revelation chapter 6, the Left Behind novels portray the seven trumpet woes as literal plagues during the first half of a seven year tribulation period.

Again, as with the seven seals, we may find out some day that the trumpet judgments were fulfilled in global warming, overfishing the oceans, species extinction, and other disasters that correspond to the symbols the Apostle John was shown in his apocalyptic vision. Or, these judgments may yet be fulfilled when God pours out his wrath at Armageddon. But, again, there is no biblical basis for asserting, as the Left Behind series does, that these judgments mean unbelievers will have a seven-year-long "second chance" after the Rapture.

Revelation 9:1-9

> And the fifth angel sounded, and I saw a star fall from heaven unto the earth; and to him was given the key of the bottomless pit. And he opened the bottomless pit, and there arose smoke out of the pit . . . And there came out of the smoke locusts upon the earth . . . And the shapes of the locusts were like horses prepared unto battle; and on their heads were, as it were, crowns like gold, and their faces were like the faces of men. And they had hair like the hair of women, and their teeth were like the teeth of lions. And they had breastplates, as it were breastplates of iron . . . (KJV)

While treating some of Revelation's signs as symbolic, the Left Behind series transforms other signs into literal events and objects. (See the discussion of Rev. 1:1 above.) So these symbolic locusts become actual realities that the novels' characters do battle with: "flying creatures— hideous, ugly, brown and black and yellow flying monsters. Swarming like locusts, they looked like miniature horses five or six inches long with tails like those of scorpions." (*Apollyon: The Destroyer Is Unleashed*, page 305) To fight them off, character Cameron ('Buck') Williams chooses a tennis racket as his weapon: "Buck snatched up the racket and stepped into a full, hard backhand, sending the locust rocketing through a window at the front of the house. The sensation of beast on strings felt as if he had smacked a toy metal car." (*Apollyon*, page 308) "Tsion taught that these were not part of the animal kingdom at all, but demons taking the form of organisms." (page 315)

Is this the historic view of the Christian Church? Far from it! For centuries Protestants understood the locusts as having reference to the Islamic armies that swept over the East. Colonial Congregationalist minister and missionary Jonathan Edwards (1703-1758) expressed it this way in *A History of the Work of Redemption*:

> "The two great works of the devil, in this space of time, against the kingdom of Christ, are his creating his Antichristian and Mahometan kingdoms; which both together comprehend the ancient Roman empire; the kingdom of Antichrist the Western, and the Mahometan kingdom the Eastern, empire. As the Scriptures in the book of Revelation represent it, it is in the destruction of these that the glorious victory of Christ, at the introduction of the glorious times of the church, will mainly consist. . . . First, the Saracens were some of his [Mohammed's] followers, who were a people of Arabia, where Mahomet lived, and who about the year seven hundred, dreadfully wasted the Roman empire.—They overran a great many countries belonging to the empire, and continued their conquests for a long time. These are supposed to be meant by the locusts mentioned in the 9th chapter of Revelation."

In his *Observations upon the Prophecies of Daniel and the Apocalypse*, originally published in 1733, Sir Isaac Newton commented similarly: "The King of these locusts was the Angel of the bottomless pit, being chief governor as well in religious as in civil affairs, such as was the Caliph of the Saracens.

Swarms of locusts often arise in Arabia felix, and from thence infest the neighbouring nations and so are a very fit type of the numerous armies of Arabians invading the Romans. They built Bagdad A.D. 766, and reigned over Persia, Syria, Arabia, Egypt, Africa and Spain." (p. 298)

Instead of seeing the locusts as a sign or symbol of invading armies, the authors of the Left Behind novels transform them into literal monstrous bugs that people must fight off with tennis rackets and whatever other weapons come to hand. But, if we are informed by the traditional understanding the Church has had throughout history, we realize that these locusts will no more fly about literally than will a literal seven-headed wild beast appear on the sea shore, as pictured in Revelation chapter 13.

Revelation 9:16-19

"And the number of the army of the horsemen were two hundred thousand thousand; and I heard the number of them. And thus I saw the horses in the vision, and them that sat on them, having breastplates of fire, and of jacinth, and brimstone; and the heads of the horses were like the heads of lions, and out of their mouths issued fire and smoke and brimstone. By these three was the third part of men killed, by the fire, and by the smoke, and by the brimstone, which issued out of their mouths. For their power is in their mouth, and in their tails; for their tails were like serpents, and had heads, and with them they do hurt." (KJV)

As mentioned above in the discussion of Revelation 1:1, the Left Behind authors ignore the fact that this is a book filled with symbolism, and instead, when the sixth trumpet sounds, they show character Rayford Steele encountering real monstrous horses. These huge beasts have actual living snakes in the place of tails, just as in John's vision. (*Assassins*, p. 127) Yet, the seven-headed beast that crawls out of the sea a few chapters later is not a real monster but merely symbolic of the evil man Nicolae Carpathia. Such inconsistency!

The historic view that prevailed in the Church for hundreds of years was to apply these verses to the invading Islamic armies that swept over the remnant of the eastern Roman Empire. Congregationalist Jonathan Edwards summed it up this way:

> "The Mahometan kingdom is another of mighty power and vast extent, set up by Satan against the kingdom of Christ. . . . And then the Turks, who were originally different from the Saracens, became followers of Mahomet, and conquered all the Eastern empire. They began their empire about the year of Christ twelve hundred and ninety-six; began to invade Europe in the year thirteen hundred; took Constantinople, and so became masters of all the Eastern empire, in the year fourteen hundred and fifty-three. And thus all the cities and countries where stood those famous churches of which we read in the New Testament, as Jerusalem, Antioch, Ephesus, Corinth, &c. now became subject to the Turks. These are supposed to be prophesied of by the horsemen in the 9th chapter of Revelation, beginning with the 15th verse." (*A History of the Work of Redemption*)

Even if we question this traditional understanding, and seek instead to apply the verses to some other episode in history, there is no biblical basis whatsoever to do as the authors of Left Behind do, and tell readers to expect these hideous horses to walk the earth literally.

Revelation 11:3-5

> "And I will give power unto my two witnesses, and they shall prophesy a thousand two hundred and threescore days, clothed in sackcloth. These are the two olive trees, and the two candlesticks standing before the God of the earth. And if any man will hurt them, fire proceedeth out of their mouth, and devoureth their enemies: and if any man will hurt them, he must in this manner be killed." (KJV)

Authors LaHaye and Jenkins identify the two witnesses as "Moses and Elijah" and state, "Readers of the Left Behind series will recognize them as the two most intriguing characters in the first five volumes." (*Are We Living in the End Times?*, pages 292-293) They are presented as leathery-skinned ancient figures who mysteriously appear on Temple Mount in Jerusalem and who preach there for 1260 days, despite repeated attempts to kill them. Character Buck Williams is granted the privilege of interviewing them for his magazine articles.

A more traditional Protestant interpretation would be to take the 1260 days as years, using the prophetic standard of "a day for a year" (Num. 14:34, Ezek. 4:6) and to understand these as Christian witnesses preaching "in sackcloth" under oppression by the papacy. Jesus declared, "ye shall be witnesses unto me both in Jerusalem, and in all Judaea, and in Samaria, and unto the uttermost part of the earth," and he spoke of the churches as "candlesticks." (Acts 1:8, Rev. 1:20 KJV) How would the 1260 years be counted? In his fascinating book *John's Revelation Unveiled* Dr. Francis Nigel Lee writes,

> "While it is difficult to set an **exact** point of departure or an exact point of fulfillment for the 1260 years of the papal desecration of the Church, it is perhaps significant that exactly 1260 years elapsed between each of the major dates in the rise of the Papacy—and each of the major dates in the decline thereof. For example: 1260 years elapsed from A.D. 257 (the first time the primacy of the Bishopric of Rome was asserted in ecclesiastical matters)—and 1517 (the time of Luther's launching of the Protestant Reformation against that primacy). Another 1260 years elapsed between the issuing of the 533 *Donation of Justinian* and its enforcement in 538 (by which the State recognized the ecclesiastical primacy of the Bishopric of Rome), and 1793 (when Romanism was abolished in France)—and 1798 (when Napoleon's General imprisoned the Pope in Rome). Another 1260 years elapsed between the decree of Emperor Phocas and the first time the Bishop of Rome alone was called 'Pope' (in 606-610)—and the Pope's loss of his last Papal State (in 1866-70)." (p. 113)

So, by several different counts, there were 1260 years of papal domination.

Albert Barnes wrote in his *Notes on the New Testament*, "The meaning of this would be, therefore, that during that long period ...there would be those who might be properly called 'witnesses' for God, and who would be engaged in holding up his truth before the world." (1884-85 edition, reprinted 1987 by Baker Book House)

Regardless of how we count the 1260 days or years, there is no sound basis for the authors of Left Behind to present the vision's "two witnesses" as two literal men, surrounded as they are by symbolism: the "seven thunders" that "spoke" in Rev. 10:4, an edible scroll (10:8-10), a "beast that comes up from the Abyss" (11:7), and a "woman clothed with the sun, with the moon under her feet." (12:1) LaHaye and Jenkins present the "woman" as symbolic, but the "men" as literal, though they are just seven verses apart in the vision; compare the discussion of Rev. 12:1-6 which follows.

Revelation 12:1-6

"A great and wondrous sign appeared in heaven: a woman clothed with the sun, with the moon under her feet and a crown of twelve stars on her head. She was pregnant and cried out in pain as she was about to give birth. Then another sign appeared in heaven: an enormous red dragon with seven heads and ten horns and seven crowns on his heads. His tail swept a third of the stars out of the sky and flung them to the earth. The dragon stood in front of the woman who was about to give birth, so that he might devour her child the moment it was born. She gave birth to a son, a male child, who will rule all the nations with an iron scepter. And her child was snatched up to God and to his throne. The woman fled into the desert to a place prepared for her by God, where she might be taken care of for 1,260 days." (NIV)

In the seventh volume of the Left Behind series, *The Indwelling*, fictional character Tsion ben Judah gets to see this scenario played out in heaven, and to question the angels Gabriel and Michael about its meaning. "'Oh! Forgive me, Prince Gabriel,' he asks. 'Can you tell me, who is the woman? Is it Mary, or is it Israel?'" Gabriel answers, "'Yes and yes.'" (p. 301)

 Applying this to Jesus' mother, as the Left Behind authors do here, would seem to be a concession to the papacy and its doctrines that have led millions to worship Mary as Queen of Heaven. Yet such an application fits nothing in the context, nor in the rest of Scripture. No wonder, then, that authors LaHaye and Jenkins go on to apply the passage primarily to Israel. She is the twelve-tribed nation that gave birth to the Messiah, and she is spoken of figuratively as a woman elsewhere in the Bible. (Compare Ezekiel 23:1-49.)

It would be difficult to disagree with *The Indwelling*'s further explanation that this means "God has prepared a place in the wilderness for his chosen people, where they too will be safe during the Great Tribulation." (p. 302) In the novels the Jews are airlifted to a desert loacation to escape the armies of Nicolae Carpathia. However, if our understanding of Matthew 24:21 is correct (see above), Jesus spoke there of a long-lasting tribulation on the Jewish people that began with the Roman siege against Jerusalem and climaxed in the Holocaust. Hitler's extermination camps operated for three and a half years (1260 days) and killed some six million Jews, but the Diaspora who lived in the Americas or in Asia, Africa or the South Pacific—all areas that Revelation's inspired writer would have considered "the wilderness"—survived. Yes, because "the woman" (Israel) had fled to "the wilderness," she truly found "a place prepared by God" to ensure the survival of the Jewish people, so that they might live to repopulate the Promised Land. These historical facts fit the passage in Revelation 12:1-6 much better than Left Behind's fiction.

A more traditional Protestant interpretation is found in Albert Barnes' *Notes on the New Testament*: "The woman representing the church. ...prophetic days, in which a day denotes a year, twelve hundred and sixty years. ...referring to the proper continuance of the Papal power, during which the true church would remain in comparative obscurity, as if driven into a desert." (1885-86 edition, reprinted in 1987 by Baker Book House) Compare the discussion of Rev. 11:3-5 above.

Either way, whether the reader sees this passage as referring to the Jewish people or the Christian church, an historical fulfillment can be found that fits perfectly. There is no need to anticipate another fulfillment during a future seven-year tribulation.

Revelation 13:1-3

> "And I stood upon the sand of the sea, and saw a beast rise up out of the sea, having seven heads and ten horns, and upon his horns ten crowns, and upon his heads the

name of blasphemy. And the beast which I saw was like a leopard, and his feet were like the feet of a bear, and his mouth like the mouth of a lion; and the dragon gave him his power, and his throne, and great authority." (KJV)

For centuries this beast has been identified with vast empires. Some students of Scripture have seen it as a composite of the beasts of Daniel's visions (Dan. 7:1 – 8:27); others, have interpreted it to mean either the pagan Roman empire or papal Rome, or both. The heads have been identified as individual emperors, or stages of Roman rule, and the ten horns as the ten nations that rose from the ruins of the empire. Albert Barnes took this position in his *Notes*:

> "The reference here is to Rome, or the one Roman power, contemplated as made up of ten subordinate kingdoms, and therefore subsequently to the invasion of the Northern hordes, and to the time when the Papacy was about to rise. . . . Thus in Daniel (vii. 2-7) the *lion* is introduced as the symbol of the Babylonian power; the bear, as the symbol of the Medo-Persian; the leopard, as the symbol of the Macedonian; and a nondescript animal, fierce, cruel, and mighty, with two horns, as the symbol of the Roman. See Notes on that passage. In John there is one animal representing the Roman power, as if it were made up of all these: a *leopard* with the feet of a *bear*, and the mouth of a *lion*, . . . and with the general description of a fierce monster. . . . the beast here represents the Roman power, as now broken up into the ten dominations which sprung up (see notes on Daniel as above) from the one original Roman power, and that became henceforward the supporters of the Papacy, and, therefore, properly represented here as having ten diadems. And upon his heads the name of blasphemy. That is, the whole power was blasphemous in its claims and pretensions."

Matthew Henry made a broader application in his *Concise Commentary on the Bible*, indicating that he saw the seven-headed beast as encompassing all the Gentile world powers from the Babylonian empire through the Roman empire—those that oppressed the Jewish church or congregation prior to Christ, as well as those that persecuted Christians:

> "It appears to mean that worldly, oppressing dominion, which for many ages, even from the times of the Babylonish captivity, had been hostile to the church. The first beast then began to

oppress and persecute the righteous for righteousness' sake, but they suffered most under the fourth beast of Daniel, (the Roman empire,) which has afflicted the saints with many cruel persecutions. The source of its power was the dragon. It was set up by the devil, and supported by him. The wounding the head may be the abolishing pagan idolatry; and the healing of the wound, introducing popish idolatry, the same in substance, only in a new dress, but which as effectually answers the devil's design. The world admired its power, policy and success. They paid honour and subjection to the devil and his instruments. It exercised infernal power and policy, requiring men to render that honour to creatures which belongs to God alone."

In contrast to these traditional writers the Left Behind novels take quite a different position. By its title, *The Indwelling: The Beast Takes Possession*, the seventh novel in the series seems to imply that the beast is Satan the devil. It shows him taking possession of and inhabiting the diabolically resurrected body of fictional world ruler Nicolae Carpathia. But the verses above make it plain that the beast is not the Devil, because "the dragon gave him his power." The dragon is "that old serpent, called the Devil and Satan" (Rev. 12:9) and he gave the beast his power, so Satan is not the beast.

And, in fact, the Left Behind authors themselves agree that Satan is not the beast, despite these implications in their seventh novel. In their nonfiction works LaHaye and Jenkins clarify that they believe the human Antichrist himself to be the beast—or at least the human Antichrist indwelt by Satan. "Satan . . . personally indwells the Antichrist and through 'the Beast' receives the worship he has always lusted after." (*Are We Living in the End Times?* p. 269) Their supporter Thomas Ice states this very clearly when he refers to "the Antichrist (also known as the Beast)." (*The Great Tribulation: Past or Future?*, p. 69) But, how could this beast be a man like the fictional character Nicolae Carpathia, rather than vast empire? The God who inspired the apostle John to write the book of Revelation was the same God who inspired the prophet Daniel to write about a series of beasts that ruled the world, picturing specific human governments. John's Jewish/Christian audience would have recognized the same metaphor. The beasts Daniel saw looked like a leopard, a bear, a lion and a fourth beast "dreadful and terrible" (Dan. 7:7), and these beasts had a total of seven heads and ten horns; John's beast was dreadful and terrible, and had the same number of heads and horns, as well as body parts of a leopard, a bear and a lion. There would be no more appropriate way to show that John's beast is a composite of Daniel's beasts—the succession of Gentile world powers all rolled into one. (See the discussion of Daniel 7:3 in this book.)

This composite beast, empowered by the dragon to rule the world, is a fitting picture of the governments Satan bragged about when he took Jesus up onto a mountain top and "showed unto him all the kingdoms of the world in a moment of time. And the devil said unto him, All this authority will I give thee, and the glory of them; for that is delivered unto me, and to whomsoever I will I give it. If thou, therefore, wilt worship me, all shall be thine." (Luke 4:5-7 KJV) Jesus rejected Satan's offer, but did not dispute the devil's role in world rulership. In fact, he regularly referred to the wicked one as "the ruler of this world" (John 12:31, 14:30, 16:11 NKJV) Satan empowered the Gentile world powers that Daniel saw as a series of beasts, including the Roman Empire that ruled the world during Jesus' earthly ministry. And Gentile powers continue to rule the world today. The composite beast John saw has been ruling the world for a long time.

By showing the devil receiving world rulership and power only through Nicolae Carpathia during a future tribulation, the authors of Left Behind minimize the power the satanic "ruler of this world" already has. This leaves readers vulnerable to his wicked influence, while they watch instead for a fictional future threat.

Revelation 13:11-14

"And I beheld another beast coming up out of the earth; and he had two horns like a lamb, and he spoke like a dragon. And he exerciseth all the power of the first beast before him, and causeth the earth and them who dwell on it to worship the first beast, whose deadly wound was healed. And he doeth great wonders, so that he maketh fire come down from heaven on the earth in the sight of men." (KJV)

The Mark, the eighth Left Behind novel, shows this two-horned beast to be a prominent individual, the fictional Leon Fortunato, right-hand man of Antichrist Nicolae Carpathia. "'Fortunato was given the power to call down fire from heaven,'" we read in the words of character David Hassid on page 130 of that volume. In their nonfiction work *Are We Living in the End Times?* LaHaye and Jenkins describe him as "the Antichrist's primary minister of propaganda, just as Goebbels was for Hitler." (p. 285)

This Left Behind interpretation, however, ignores all of the evidence that the "beasts" in Revelation mirror the "beasts" in Daniel, which the Hebrew prophet clearly identified as kingdoms or governments. (Compare the discussions of Daniel 7:3 and Revelation 13:1-3 above.)

Commenting on this beast from the earth, Jonathan Edwards (1703-1758) wrote, "This also designates the church of Rome. Fire coming down from heaven, seems to have reference to their excommunications, which were dreaded like fire from heaven." (*A History of the Work of Redemption*) Even medieval kings quaked in fear at the threat of being excommunicated by the pope.

Matthew Henry's Commentary says, "Those who think the first beast signifies Rome pagan by this second beast would understand Rome papal, which promotes idolatry and tyranny, but in a more soft and lamb-like manner: those that understand the first beast of the secular power of the papacy take the second to intend its spiritual and ecclesiastical powers, which act under the disguise of religion and charity to the souls of men."

Martin Luther took the first position Matthew Henry mentioned, declaring as follows: "Here, then, are the two Beasts. The one is the Empire. The other, with the two horns, is the Papacy." (Luther's *Second Preface to the Revelation of St. John* in *Works* VI:484, translated by Dr. F. N. Lee)

Some modern writers have noted that man's governments today are literally able to 'make fire come down from heaven' by waging war with planes and rockets. So they see a possible fulfillment in events and entities that have come onto the world scene long after the classic Reformation and post-Reformation writers passed away. Which world power first dropped nuclear bombs from the sky? Which power is well known for calling down flaming napalm upon targets in Vietnam? The Anglo world power, led by its two horns, Britain and America, changed the world by promoting the ideals of democracy and freedom. Hence it looks like a lamb compared to other empires, but it also speaks like a dragon. These factors alone would make it a possible candidate for the two-horned beast, but even more important is the English-speaking combo's role in the creation of "the image of the beast," as discussed below. Steve Wohlberg, author of the books *Truth Left Behind* and *The Left Behind Deception* suggests in his article "America in Bible Prophecy" that "America is the exact power specifically mentioned in this mysterious verse." See his EndTimeInsights.com web site at https://www.endtimeinsights.com/site/v2_3/index.php?option=com_content&task=view&id=13&Itemid=63

Whether the passage really applies to the power of the papacy or to a modern superpower, there is no sound basis for applying it to a future fictional character like Left Behind's Leon Fortunato. To be consistent with the rest of the beasts in Daniel and Revelation, the 'beast coming up out of the earth' must be a kingdom or government—not an individual man.

Revelation 13:15

"...saying to them that dwell on the earth, that they should make an image to the beast...And he hath power to give life unto the image of the beast, that the image of the beast should both speak, and cause that as many as would not worship the image of the beast should be killed." (KJV)

In his *Notes on the New Testament* Albert Barnes identifies the image as papal Rome: "All that is stated here would be fulfilled if the old Roman civil power should become to a large extent dead, or cease to exert its influence over men, and if then the Papal spiritual power should cause a form of domination to exist, *strongly resembling* the former in its general character and extent, and if it should secure this result—that the world would acknowledge its sway or render it homage as it did to the old Roman government." In this view papal Rome is the image of the beast, the image imperial Rome.

Other writers see the pope as the two-horned beast from the earth, spoken of above in Revelation 13:11, imparting power to a revived Roman empire under Charlemagne; this new Holy Roman Empire would then be the image of the old imperial Rome. Martin Luther wrote, "the Papacy . . . has now become a temporal Kingdom yet with the reputation and Name of Christ . . . The Pope restored the fallen Roman Empire. . . . It is an image of the Roman Empire, rather than the body of the Empire as it once was. Nevertheless, he puts spirit and life into this image . . . and actually operates it to some extent. This is the image [of that] which was wounded, but did live." (Luther's *Second Preface to the Revelation of St. John* in *Works* VI:484, translated by Dr. F. N. Lee) The Holy Roman Empire (German: *Heiliges Römisches Reich*), with emperors crowned by the Roman pope for hundreds of years, also came to be called the Holy Roman Empire of the German Nation (*Heiliges Römisches Reich Deutscher Nation*). Its borders expanded and contracted over the centuries as conflicts were won and lost and as political alliances were forged. It was this "Reich" or Empire that Adolph Hitler referred to when dubbing his Nazi government the *Third* Reich and seeking to reclaim lost territory. Under this incarnation of the Empire, it was true that those who would not render worship through the Seig Heil salute were literally killed.

Some modern writers who take an historicist approach to Bible prophecy see the United Nations organization as a fulfillment of the image of the beast. Since the U.N. did not come into existence until some four hundred years after the Reformation, the Reformers could hardly be expected to know about it. But did God foresee it and inspire John to write about it? As noted in the discussions of Revelation 13:1-3 and 13:11-14, and the earlier consideration of Daniel 7:3, "beasts" are symbolic of kingdoms, governments and Gentile world powers that interact with God's people down through history from the time of ancient Israel through the return of Christ. The seven-headed, ten-horned beast of Revelation 13:1, that has parts resembling a leopard, a bear and a lion, is a composite of the separate beasts Daniel described, whose heads added up to seven, with a total of ten horns. Daniel explained that his individual beasts represented a succession of kingdoms. (Dan. 7:17, 23) So, could the "image" of the composite "beast" be some sort of miniature organizational replica of the Gentile world powers—like the United Nations? Before the twentieth century it would have been difficult to imagine how the nations could make an "image" of the world's governments—much less cause such an image to take on a life of its own. But today we have such a living, breathing image with its headquarters on the shore of the East River in New York City. The United Nations organization certainly can be seen as a mirror image of the kingdoms of this world, a miniature replica of the planet's political structure. The successors of the kingdoms Daniel wrote about—Babylon (Iraq), Persia (Iran), Greece and Rome (Italy)—are all represented, as well as the rest of the nations of this world. And this organizational image of the world's governments has taken on a life of its own, so that it "speaks" though official Resolutions and causes those resolutions to be enforced, ultimately through military action when necessary. Those who fail to bow to its authority may indeed be killed.

Although the United Nations organization takes a prominent role in the Left Behind novels, authors LaHaye and Jenkins take quite a different approach. They abandon the long-held understanding of "beasts" as representing governments or world powers, and instead present the man Nicolae Carpathia as the beast of Revelation chapter 13. His appointment as Secretary General of the United Nations marks the beginning of his rise to power as the Antichrist. So the image of the beast must then be a statue of this man.. In *The Indwelling*, the seventh novel in the series, temperamental sculptor Guy Blod, the one-world government's Minister of the Creative Arts, is commissioned to create a metal statue, in his words "a sort of bronzy iron thingie of Nicolae" Carpathia, the recently assassinated Antichrist. (p. 60) The artist himself is taken by surprise when the metal monstrosity begins to speak with Carpathia's voice. (p. 285) Is this statue of a dead dictator's naked body really what God had in mind when he inspired the Apostle John to write about "the image of the beast"?

No, the use of 'beasts' in scriptural imagery consistently to represent governments—whether imperial Rome or papal power or a revived Roman empire or other Gentile world powers—argues against Left Behind's attempt to find fulfillment of this passage in "a sort of bronzy iron thingie" of Nicolae Carpathia.

Revelation 13:16-17

"He also forced everyone, small and great, rich and poor, free and slave, to receive a mark on his right hand or on his forehead, so that no one could buy or sell unless he had the mark, which is the name of the beast or the number of his name." (NIV)

In the Left Behind novels the "mark" is a literal tattoo-like marking inscribed on the forehead or on the hand of all who submit to Nicolae Carpathia, Tim LaHaye's "beast" and "Antichrist." The novels portray a situation where "the Antichrist will have total control of the world's economy during the last three years of the Tribulation." (*Are We Living in the End Times?*, p. 195) Since the mark is required for employment and for financial transactions, Christian characters set up an underground economy based on bartering goods and services.

In contrast to this view, *Matthew Henry's Commentary* provides a traditional Protestant interpretation:

> "It is probable that *the mark, the name,* and *the number of the beast,* may all signify the same thing—that they make an open profession of their subjection and obedience to the papacy, which is receiving the mark in their forehead, and that they oblige themselves to use all their interest, power, and endeavour, to promote the papal authority, which is receiving the mark in their right hands. We are told that pope Martin V. in his bull, added to the council of Constance, prohibits Roman catholics from suffering any heretics to dwell in their countries, or to make any bargains, use any trades, or bear any civil offices, which is a very clear interpretation of this prophecy."

So, according to the traditional understanding, the mark refers to loyal support of the papal antichrist, rather than any visible tattoo. Such support and obedience was required for anyone wishing to "buy or sell" in Catholic lands during the height of papal power.

According to other interpretations of the beast and its image, fulfillment of this passage could refer to other situations where governments have required loyalty and obedience as a prerequisite to doing business. Historically, Christians have already faced such times of testing in many lands. Christians who failed to show loyalty to Hitler and his Nazi party lost their jobs in Germany and in occupied Europe under the Third Reich, which, as noted above, saw itself as a revival of the Holy Roman Empire that Martin Luther identified as the image of the beast. Totalitarian Communist governments have imposed similar economic hardships on believers. A billion people today live in China, and another billion in Muslim lands, where an open expression of faith in Christ can bring severe economic punishment.

It would be a shame to allow Left Behind's speculation about a supposed future fulfillment to distract us from the real-world challenges Christians have faced in the past and currently face in much of the world today—the temptation to compromise their faith in order to be able to "buy or sell."

Revelation 15:1

> "I saw in heaven another great and marvelous sign: seven angels with the seven last plagues—last, because with them God's wrath is completed." (NIV)

John said this was another "sign"—something symbolic—but the Left Behind novels go on to present these last plagues as quite literal. Painful sores literally break out on people, the sea and the rivers actually turn to blood, people are scorched by intense heat, and so on. Please compare the discussion of Revelation 1:1, above, for a more appropriate way to view such symbolism.

Revelation 17:3-9, 18

> "I saw a woman sitting on a scarlet beast that was covered with blasphemous names and had seven heads and ten horns. ...This title was written on her forehead:
>
> MYSTERY
>
> BABYLON THE GREAT
>
> THE MOTHER OF PROSTITUTES
>
> AND OF THE ABOMINATIONS OF THE EARTH.
>
> I saw that the woman was drunk with the blood of the saints, the blood of those who bore testimony to Jesus. ... Then the angel said to me: '... I will explain to you the mystery of the woman and of the beast she rides, which has the seven heads and ten horns. ...The seven heads are seven hills on which the woman sits. ... The woman you saw is the great city that rules over the kings of the earth.'" (NIV)

Much of the action in the Left Behind novels centers around the city of Babylon, rebuilt on its ancient site in Iraq during the seven-year tribulation by Global Community Potentate (and Antichrist) Nicolae Carpathia. Once a great seat of empire in the days of Nebuchadnezzar and the prophet Daniel, Babylon fell and never regained prominence. Must it be rebuilt by the Antichrist, in order for Bible prophecy to be fulfilled? Along with the seven-year tribulation, this concept, too, has gained popularity in recent decades, with its greatest boost coming from the end times fiction of the Left Behind series.

Authors LaHaye and Jenkins wrote for a generation that waged two wars against Saddam Hussein, Iraq's leader who spent vast sums restoring the antiquities of Babylon and who identified himself as a modern Nebuchadnezzar. However, the Apostle John wrote his Apocalypse for a different audience. The Word of God is timeless and inspired by God to benefit readers throughout the centuries, but a proper understanding of Scripture always begins with recognition of the contemporary audience and what the passage meant to them.

The First Century readers addressed by the Apostle John most certainly understood that he was not predicting a restoration of an ancient Mesopotamian city. They recognized "Babylon" as a code name for Rome. Why? Because the coins they carried in their purses displayed the very same symbols John described in the verses above. The currency in John's day bore the image and inscription of Emperor Vespasian, but on the reverse side the coins displayed a woman sitting on seven hills, with the caption "ROMA" identifying her. Such coins were minted during Vespasian's reign, from 69 to 79 A.D., and the symbols on them would have been as familiar to John's audience as George Washington's face on the dollar bill is to modern Americans. (See pages 104-107 of the book *Iraq: Babylon of the End-Times?* by C. Marvin Pate and J. Daniel Hays, Baker Book House, 2003) Rome of John's day sat on seven hills, was drunk with the blood of the saints who bore witness to Jesus, and was the great city that ruled over the kings of the earth. We need not look any farther to know which city John meant when he wrote these words in his Apocalypse.

Although John clearly had pagan Rome in mind, could it be that the Holy Spirit who inspired him intended more than that? Many writers see prophetic application also to ecclesiastical Rome, which came to rule over much of the world at the height of papal power, which sat on the same seven hills, and which became drunk with the blood of Bible-believing saints during the Inquisition. Of this blood-bath, Spurgeon wrote, "All churches, when they lose the spirit of Christ, are very prone to persecute; but a horrible pre-eminence must be awarded to the scarlet harlot of the seven hills, for no church on earth except that of Rome has had a separate institution for hunting out and destroying heretics." ("The Inquisition" by C. H. Spurgeon, from the August 1868 *Sword and Trowel* magazine, available online at www.Spurgeon.org/s_and_t/inq.htm)

The pope inherited the title *Pontifex Maximus* (today often shortened to 'Pontiff') from the ancient pagan Roman priesthood and from the Caesars who later took the title upon themselves. Extensive parallels have also been drawn between the trappings of the papacy and ancient Babylonian religious worship. The Reformers make it clear in their writings that there is no biblical basis for a powerful pope hailed as 'the vicar of Christ,' a hierarchy of celibate priests, monks and nuns, veneration of saints, miracles attributed to bones and other relics, and so on. The crass sale of indulgences has ceased, in the light of Martin Luther's objections, but the hierarchy still extracts payment for masses supposedly needed to free dead loved ones from the torments of purgatory. When ancient Jerusalem proved unfaithful, God inspired Isaiah to write that "the faithful city has become a harlot" (Isa. 1:21), so similar language could be expected regarding papal Rome.

Moreover, the church of Rome can indeed be called "the mother of prostitutes." Some of her daughter denominations and churches, while abandoning the open abuses of the papacy, have nonetheless prostituted themselves by relying on the theories of 'science' and sociology instead of on the written Word of God, and by welcoming fornication, adultery and homosexual practice among their members and even their clergy.

Whether Revelation chapters 17 and 18 speak of imperial Rome or of papal Rome—or both—there is no basis in Scripture for insisting as do the authors of *Left Behind* that the Apocalypse requires a rebuilt Babylon to become the world capital during the end times.

Revelation 18:1-2, 21, 24

> another angel coming down from heaven... shouted: "Fallen! Fallen is Babylon the Great! ...
>
> Then a mighty angel picked up a boulder the size of a large millstone and threw it into the sea, and said:

> "With such violence the great city of Babylon will be thrown down, never to be found again... In her was found the blood of prophets and of the saints, and of all who have been killed on the earth." (NIV)

Ancient Babylon must be rebuilt, so say *Left Behind*'s authors LaHaye and Jenkins: "Since the word 'fallen' is used twice in each of these passages, the rabbinic rule demands that the city fall twice. But if it is to fall again, it must first be rebuilt." (*Are We Living in the End Times?* page 138) However, we can be sure that the Apostle John did not feel bound by the "ancient rabbinic rule of interpretation" that they cite. Rather, as noted above in the discussion of Revelation 17:3-9 and 18, John was clearly writing about Rome, not about ancient Babylon or an end-times reconstruction of that great city.

Conclusion

As noted above, Tim LaHaye and Jerry Jenkins believe that the events they portrayed in the Left Behind novels actually "will happen someday." They wrote the books, not to entertain readers, but to present "the truth of end times prophecy in fiction form." (*Kingdom Come: The Final Victory*, pages 355-356) We have seen, however, that their presentation departs from the understanding Bible readers have held for centuries and contradicts Christ's teaching.

Jesus never taught that unbelievers would be 'left behind' for a seven-year-long 'second chance' when he returns. The verse-by-verse discussions in this book show that his coming will be like the days of Noah when eight people entered the safety of the Ark and the wicked world was swept away, and like the days of Lot when that righteous man's family was led to safety while the cities of Sodom and Gomorrah were burnt up. Jesus' parables and plain teaching make it clear that we must "keep watch, because you do not know on what day your Lord will come." (Matt. 24:42 NIV) His coming will be as it was in the days of Noah and in the days of Lot.

The Left Behind novels tell a different story. They show half-hearted occasional churchgoers like Rayford Steele and hypocritical unbelieving clergymen like Bruce Barnes left behind with a second chance—seven more years to make up their minds about Christ. This teaching is not biblical.

Moreover, as has been shown above, the 'left behind' scenario was unknown among Bible-believers down through the centuries. Tyndale, Huss, Wycliffe, Knox, Calvin, Luther, Wesley, Spurgeon and the others quoted in this book were serious students of the Word of God, but they never encountered in Scripture a two-stage return of Christ that would give unbelievers a seven-year reprieve. The founders of the Baptist, Presbyterian, Calvinist, Congregationalist, Lutheran and Reformed traditions would not recognize the beliefs that millions of their nominal adherents today have learned from the popular novels by LaHaye and Jenkins.

By the same token today's churchgoers are largely ignorant of the traditional Protestant understanding of end times prophecy. Hence they are oblivious to the warnings that all the great preachers of the past gave concerning the apostasy, the man of sin, and the antichrist that arose from the ruins of the Roman Empire—entities that continue to lead much of the world's population away from Christ. These enemies of God are seldom named from pulpits today, but they are clearly identified in the quotes featured throughout this book.

During the late 1800's and early 1900's the contrary teachings of John Nelson Darby were quietly adopted by one theology professor and then another, by one seminary and then another, by one church and then another, by one denomination and then another. Protestants learned to put off the prophecies until a supposed future Tribulation. It was more 'politically correct' to accept Islam and the papacy as acceptable alternative viewpoints, and to discard the embarrassing accusations that filled the writings of the Reformation. Now that a couple more generations have passed, the teaching of the Reformers has been so completely forgotten that it is foreign to the thinking of both the pulpit and the pew.

If the Left Behind scenario is wrong, does that mean the excitement about end times prophecy that the novels have stimulated is also wrong? Far from it! Rather, there is every reason to believe that our Redeemer's coming is imminent. The history of divine intervention in ages past identifies the types of situations that provoke God to act. The flood of Noah's day was sent to cleanse a planet that had become full of sexual immorality and violence, much like today's world. Surely this age of internet pornography, motion picture sex goddesses, and weapons of mass destruction tries the Creator's patience to its limits. If God sent fire and brimstone to destroy Sodom and Gomorrah, when the homosexual practices of those towns brought an outcry to his ears, how much longer will he put up with the open gay pride movement that is spreading like wildfire today, and the world that welcomes it with hardly a cry of complaint? When the builders of the Tower of Babel abandoned God to create an urban society capable of accomplishing the impossible, He stopped them in their tracks. So, what about today's predominantly urban world that boasts of human achievement and looks to science to solve all man's problems? How much farther will God let this world go in crediting blind evolution for the Creator's handiwork, developing nuclear weapons, manipulating the genome, and performing sex-change operations? The One who put a stop to Babel, to Sodom and to the pre-Flood world will soon put a stop to today's antichristian culture—this time through the promised return of his Son.

The failings of Left Behind do not in any way negate the scriptural injunctions to "keep watch" and "look forward to the day of God." (Matt. 25:13; 2 Pet. 3:12 NIV) Without Left Behind's promise of a 'second chance,' that biblical warning is to be taken even more seriously.

The seven-year struggle of the Left Behind characters Cameron Williams and Rayford Steele against Antichrist Nicolae Carpathia is fast-moving, and therefore captivates modern audiences accustomed to such dramatic action on television and at the movies. But, what about the centuries-long struggle of real-world Christians against the dark forces Martin Luther and John Calvin identified as the real Antichrist? That true story may not be as fast moving, but we should recall that "with the Lord a day is like a thousand years, and a thousand years are like a day." (2 Pet. 3:8 NIV) In fact, the real-life history of this struggle is even more fascinating than the Left Behind novels. Take the time to read about how John Huss was burned at the stake for preaching the truth. Read how William Tyndale was killed for translating the Bible and standing up to the Antichrist. Read about modern-day Muslim men and women who learn the Gospel message and embrace Jesus Christ as their Savior and Lord, only to be jailed, abused, stoned or beheaded in strict Islamic nations today.

Unfortunately, the Left Behind novels have validated unbelievers' "wait and see" attitude by assuring them of seven more years to get right with God after Christ returns. While the novelists urge their readers to accept Christ *now* rather than later, they undermine this by offering a future tribulation period as a seven-year safety net. If the penalty for postponing a personal decision about Christ is nothing worse than a seven-year adventure after his coming, why worry?

However, if the traditional understanding of the Second Coming turns out to be correct, and Christ raptures the Church as he metes out swift punishment to the rest of the world, the undecided who relied on Left Behind's interpretation may be in for an unpleasant surprise with eternal consequences.

Bibliography

Left Behind series fiction

Left Behind: A Novel of the Earth's Last Days, (No. 1) Tim LaHaye and Jerry B. Jenkins (Tyndale, 1995)

Tribulation Force: The Continuing Drama of those Left Behind (No. 2), Tim LaHaye and Jerry B. Jenkins (Tyndale, 1996)

Nicolae: The Rise of Antichrist (No. 3), Tim LaHaye and Jerry B. Jenkins (Tyndale, 1997)

Soul Harvest: The World Takes Sides (No. 4), Tim LaHaye and Jerry B. Jenkins (Tyndale, 1998)

Apollyon: The Destroyer Is Unleashed (No. 5), Tim LaHaye and Jerry B. Jenkins (Tyndale, 1999)

Assassins: Assignment: Jerusalem, Target: Antichrist (No. 6), Tim LaHaye and Jerry B. Jenkins (Tyndale, 1999)

The Indwelling: The Beast Takes Possession (No. 7), Tim LaHaye and Jerry B. Jenkins (Tyndale, 2000)

The Mark: The Beast Rules the World (No. 8), Tim LaHaye and Jerry B. Jenkins (Tyndale, 2000)

Desecration: Antichrist Takes the Throne (No. 9), Tim LaHaye and Jerry B. Jenkins (Tyndale, 2001)

The Remnant: On the Brink of Armageddon (No. 10), Tim LaHaye and Jerry B. Jenkins (Tyndale, 2002)

Armageddon: The Cosmic Battle of the Ages (No. 11), Tim LaHaye and Jerry B. Jenkins (Tyndale, 2003)

Glorious Appearing: The End of Days (No. 12), Tim LaHaye and Jerry B. Jenkins (Tyndale, 2004)

Kingdom Come: The Final Victory (No. 13) , Tim LaHaye and Jerry B. Jenkins (Tyndale, 2007)

PREQUELS:

The Rising: Antichrist Is Born – Before They Were Left Behind, Tim LaHaye and Jerry B. Jenkins (Tyndale, 2005)

The Regime: Evil Advances – Before They Were Left Behind, Tim LaHaye and Jerry B. Jenkins (Tyndale, 2005)

The Rapture: In the Twinkling of an Eye – Before They Were Left Behind, Tim LaHaye and Jerry B. Jenkins (Tyndale, 2006)

THE KIDS:

The Vanishings: Four Kids Face Earth's Last Days Together – Left Behind: The Kids (No. 1), Jerry B. Jenkins and Tim LaHaye (Tyndale, 1998)

Second Chance: The Search for Truth – Left Behind: The Kids (No. 2), Jerry B. Jenkins and Tim LaHaye (Tyndale, 1998)

Through the Flames: The Kids Risk Their Lives – Left Behind: The Kids (No. 3), Jerry B. Jenkins and Tim LaHaye (Tyndale, 1998)

Facing the FutureX – Left Behind: The Kids (No. 4), Jerry B. Jenkins and Tim LaHaye (Tyndale, 1998)

Nicolae High – Left Behind: The Kids (No. 5), Jerry B. Jenkins and Tim LaHaye (Tyndale, 1999)

The Underground – Left Behind: The Kids (No. 6), Jerry B. Jenkins and Tim LaHaye (Tyndale, 1999)

Busted! – Left Behind: The Kids (No. 7), Jerry B. Jenkins and Tim LaHaye (Tyndale, 2000)

Death Strike – Left Behind: The Kids (No. 8), Jerry B. Jenkins and Tim LaHaye (Tyndale, 2000)

The Search – Left Behind: The Kids (No. 9), Jerry B. Jenkins and Tim LaHaye (Tyndale, 2000)

On the Run – Left Behind: The Kids (No. 10), Jerry B. Jenkins and Tim LaHaye (Tyndale, 2000)

Into the Storm – Left Behind: The Kids (No. 11), Jerry B. Jenkins and Tim LaHaye (Tyndale, 2000)

Earthquake – Left Behind: The Kids (No. 12), Jerry B. Jenkins and Tim

LaHaye (Tyndale, 2000)

The Showdown – Left Behind: The Kids (No. 13), Jerry B. Jenkins and Tim LaHaye (Tyndale, 2001)

Judgment Day – Left Behind: The Kids (No. 14), Jerry B. Jenkins and Tim LaHaye (Tyndale, 2001)

Battling the Commander – Left Behind: The Kids (No. 15), Jerry B. Jenkins and Tim LaHaye (Tyndale, 2001)

Fire from Heaven – Left Behind: The Kids (No. 16), Jerry B. Jenkins and Tim LaHaye (Tyndale, 2001)

Terror in the Stadium – Left Behind: The Kids (No. 17), Jerry B. Jenkins and Tim LaHaye (Tyndale, 2001)

Darkening Skies – Left Behind: The Kids (No. 18), Jerry B. Jenkins and Tim LaHaye (Tyndale, 2001)

The Attack of Apollyon – Left Behind: The Kids (No. 19), Jerry B. Jenkins and Tim LaHaye (Tyndale, 2002)

A Dangerous Plan – Left Behind: The Kids (No. 20), Jerry B. Jenkins and Tim LaHaye (Tyndale, 2002)

Secrets of New Babylon – Left Behind: The Kids (No. 21), Jerry B. Jenkins and Tim LaHaye (Tyndale, 2002)

Escape from New Babylon – Left Behind: The Kids (No. 22), Jerry B. Jenkins and Tim LaHaye (Tyndale, 2002)

Horsemen of Terror – Left Behind: The Kids (No. 23), Jerry B. Jenkins and Tim LaHaye (Tyndale, 2002)

Uplink from the Underground – Left Behind: The Kids (No. 24), Jerry B. Jenkins and Tim LaHaye (Tyndale, 2002)

Death at the Gala – Left Behind: The Kids (No. 25), Jerry B. Jenkins and Tim LaHaye (Tyndale, 2003)

The Beast Arises – Left Behind: The Kids (No. 26), Jerry B. Jenkins and Tim LaHaye (Tyndale, 2003)

Wildfire! – Left Behind: The Kids (No. 27), Jerry B. Jenkins and Tim LaHaye (Tyndale, 2003)

The Mark of the Beast – Left Behind: The Kids (No. 28), Jerry B. Jenkins and Tim LaHaye (Tyndale, 2003)

Breakout! – Left Behind: The Kids (No. 29), Jerry B. Jenkins and Tim LaHaye (Tyndale, 2003)

Murder in the Holy Place – Left Behind: The Kids (No. 30), Jerry B. Jenkins and Tim LaHaye (Tyndale, 2003)

Escape to Masada – Left Behind: The Kids (No. 31), Jerry B. Jenkins and Tim LaHaye (Tyndale, 2003)

War of the Dragon – Left Behind: The Kids (No. 32), Jerry B. Jenkins and Tim LaHaye (Tyndale, 2003)

Attack on Petra – Left Behind: The Kids (No. 33), Jerry B. Jenkins and Tim LaHaye (Tyndale, 2004)

Bounty Hunters – Left Behind: The Kids (No. 34), Jerry B. Jenkins and Tim LaHaye (Tyndale, 2004)

The Rise of False Messiahs – Left Behind: The Kids (No. 35), Jerry B. Jenkins and Tim LaHaye (Tyndale, 2004)

Ominous Choices – Left Behind: The Kids (No. 36), Jerry B. Jenkins and Tim LaHaye (Tyndale, 2004)

Heat Wave – Left Behind: The Kids (No. 37), Jerry B. Jenkins and Tim LaHaye (Tyndale, 2004)

The Perils of Love – Left Behind: The Kids (No. 38), Jerry B. Jenkins and Tim LaHaye (Tyndale, 2004)

The Road to War – Left Behind: The Kids (No. 39), Jerry B. Jenkins and Tim LaHaye (Tyndale, 2004)

Triumphant Return – Left Behind: The Kids (No. 40), Jerry B. Jenkins and Tim LaHaye (Tyndale, 2004)

Nonfiction books

Are We Living in the End Times? Tim LaHaye and Jerry B. Jenkins (Tyndale, 1999)

Backgrounds to Dispensationalism: Its Historical Genesis and Ecclesiastical Implications Clarence B. Bass (Wm. B. Eerdmans Publishing Company, 1960)

End Times Fiction: A Biblical Consideration of the Left Behind Theology, Gary DeMar (Thomas Nelson Publishers, 2001)

Four Views on the Book of Revelation, Kenneth L. Gentry Jr., Sam Hamstra Jr., C. Marvin Pate and Robert L. Thomas (Zondervan, 1998)

Iraq: Babylon of the End-Times?, C. Marvin Pate and J. Daniel Hays (Baker Books, 2003)

John's Revelation Unveiled, Francis Nigel Lee (The Historicism Research Foundation, 2001)

Matthew Henry's Concise Commentary on the Bible, Matthew Henry, et al. (1721, on the Internet in the Christian Classics Ethereal Library collection at www.CCEL.org)

Matthew Henry's Commentary on the Whole Bible, Matthew Henry, et al. (1706-1721, reprinted by MacDonald Publishing Company, also on the Internet in the Christian Classics Ethereal Library collection at www.CCEL.org)

New Scofield Reference Bible, The, C. I. Scofield editor (New York: Oxford University Press, original date of publication 1909, 1967 edition)

Notes on the New Testament, Albert Barnes (1884-1885 edition, reprinted by Baker Book House, 1987; also on the Internet in the Christian Classics Ethereal Library collection at www.CCEL.org)

Nobody Left Behind: Insight into "End-Time" Prophecies, David Vaughn Elliott (self-published, 2004)

Observations Upon the Prophecies of Daniel and the Apocalypse, Sir Isaac Newton (Printland edition, 1998)

Rapture Under Attack Tim LaHaye (Multnomah, 1998) [originally published as *No Fear of the Storm* in 1992]

The Great Tribulation: Past or Future?, Thomas Ice and Kenneth L. Gentry Jr. (Kregel Publications, 1999)

The Left Behind Deception: Revealing Dangerous Errors about the Rapture and the Antichrist, Steve Wohlberg (Remnant Publications, 2001)

The Truth Behind Left Behind, Mark Hitchcock and Thomas Ice (Multnomah, 2004)

The Works of Jonathan Edwards with a Memoir by Sereno E. Dwight, Revised and Corrected by Edward Hickman, Volume One, Part IV (1834, reprinted 1995 by Banner of Truth Trust) ; also on the Internet in the Christian Classics Ethereal Library collection at www.CCEL.org)

Three Views on the Rapture: Pre-, Mid-, or Post-Tribulation, Gleason L. Archer Jr., Paul D. Feinberg, Douglas J. Moo and Richard R. Reiter (Zondervan, 1996)

Truth Left Behind: Exposing End-Time Errors about the Rapture and the

Antichrist, Steve Wohlberg (Pacific Press Publishing Association, 2001)

Articles

"America in Bible Prophecy" by Steve Wohlberg at https://www.endtimeinsights.com/site/v2_3/index.php?option=com_c ontent&task=view&id=13&Itemid=63

"Antichrist in the Early Church" by William C. Weinrich in the April/July 1985 issue of *Concordia Theological Quarterly*

"Calvin on Islam" by Rev. Dr. Prof. Francis Nigel Lee at http://www.dr-fnlee.org/docs6/calvislam/calvislam.pdf

"Luther on Islam and the Papacy" by Rev. Dr. Prof. Francis Nigel Lee at http://www.dr-fnlee.org/docs/loiatp/loiatp.pdf

"The Inquisition" by C. H. Spurgeon, from the August 1868 *Sword and Trowel* magazine at http://www.Spurgeon.org/s_and_t/inq.htm

RESEARCHER David A. Reed served for a decade as a contributing editor of Dr. Walter Martin's *Christian Research Journal*, while also editing his own counter-cult periodical *Comments from the Friends*. He has authored more than a dozen books on Bible topics including *Blood on the Altar* (Prometheus Books) and the popular *Jehovah's Witnesses Answered Verse by Verse* and *Mormons Answered Verse by Verse* (Baker Book House). Known world-wide as an expert on the failed prophecies of the cults, Reed has spent recent years looking closer to home, researching the prophetic teachings of Protestant churches today, as well as the Reformation teachings of Luther, Calvin, Wycliffe, Wesley and Spurgeon that were tossed aside to make room for today's popular Left Behind theology. David and his wife Penni are active members of a three hundred year old church in Plymouth County, Massachusetts. Reed's web sites include AnswerJW.com and LeftBehindAnswered.com.